"This book combines the nu
with often undervalued but c
budding entrepreneurs with
the entrepreneurial journey.   ......ors have
been there and done that makes for a reassuring, enlightening
and transformative read. I will definitely be sharing this with my
students and placing it at the very top of their reading list!"
LJ Silverman, Head of LSE Generate,
LSE Research & Innovation

"One of the biggest challenges with starting a business is
growing it. *Humble Crumbles* is very relevant in building the
sort of leadership that the world requires, especially in these
very uncertain times. Every chapter is well-crafted to provoke
and inspire long-term thinking. I highly recommend this book
to individuals who want to become more visionary in their
entrepreneurial journey."
Samuel T Reddy, Speaker; Impact Entrepreneur; and Author
of *Leavers to Leaders: Seven Steps to Reinvent Yourself While*
in Transition

"*Humble Crumbles* is *the* book for existing and prospective
entrepreneurs. Combining the practical with the analytical, Paul
and Sylvana have written a concise desktop companion for the
e-class, which can and should be used as a guidepost throughout
the adventure. A work of candour, humility, humour and
accountability, it's a refreshing read that should become a staple
for academic and professional audiences alike."
Mike Wilson, Senior Advisor and Board Member, Horizon8

"A gem of a management book; a must-read for budding entrepreneurs. Refreshingly, it is not a book of 'Management Theory', but one based on personal and practical experience and failure. We should all learn from our mistakes but, all too often, by inclination or obstinance, we repeat ourselves. Paul and Sylvana have the wisdom and hindsight to analyse their own mistakes and share their hard-earned experience. The result is an easy-to-read book that synthesises much valuable knowledge of actually HOW to go about launching a successful new business."
Daniel A Pouget, EIR (Entrepreneur-in-Residence) at INSEAD; NED and Former Senior Partner CEO, DLP James Capel Stockbrokers; Former Managing Director, Nasdaq Europe

"In *Humble Crumbles* you will experience a vastly different business book, which in many ways is almost a modern version of a Greek play, transplanted into the world of the entrepreneur. The feast that awaits you is a rich mixture of insights, humour and pathos leavened by great pearls of wisdom. Throughout an easy-to-read and sometimes light-hearted dialogue, you are a silent partner in a conversation between two experts. They tell a fascinating story of the rise and fall of an idea and a brand. At the same time, they share knowledge and advice informed by life's lessons as well as by the expertise of a highly trained executive coach. The end-game of these experts is to help you consider how your personality, your values, your decisions and the people whom you trust shape the outcomes and the ultimate fate of your enterprise."
Edna Kissman, Social Entrepreneur; Founder and CEO at The Wonder of Me

"Storylines, particularly based on real-life experiences, are so much more powerful to me when coupled with lessons learnt, lightbulb moments and the honest acknowledgement of mistakes. Such it is with this wonderful recount told through the complimentary skills, talent and experiences of Paul O'Donnell and Sylvana Caloni. Regardless of the industry, this book should be in the library of all contemplating or embarking upon the entrepreneurial experience."

PH Cunningham, Independent Director, Professional Investment Advisory Services Pte Ltd Singapore

"I absolutely love this book – read it from cover to cover in one sitting. The fact that Sylvana and Paul have written such an easy-to-read book demonstrates their knack for getting to key issues that face all entrepreneurs, from idea, or 'lightbulb moment', to ultimate success or closure of the business. It is a book that I will be sharing with every aspiring entrepreneur I know, as I am confident it will help them avoid some of the pitfalls of creating one's own business. The book's framework is well thought out and the angles taken by Paul and Sylvana are exactly what I have seen happen in real life. I particularly like the 'Crumbs of Wisdom' at the end of each chapter, which when listed out in full make a great 'how to' guide for leaders of new businesses. This book is a must-read for anyone thinking about starting a business. It even shows us that when things do not go to plan and your dream business dissolves, you can still emerge stronger, feeling good about what you did, and retain your sense of humour."

Jeannette Lichner, Non-Executive Director; Executive Coach and Leadership Tutor

"In running a small business, I am learning over and over again that it is not just about the 'how', it is the 'who' that is just as important: the self-awareness, listening, balancing realism with enthusiasm, managing expectations, and managing myself. *Humble Crumbles* is a concise but dense coverage of both the 'how' and 'who', that I will be coming back to over and over to pick up another idea, gain a new perspective, and to review the advice from a new understanding, as my own experience and knowledge progresses."

Victoria Silberbauer, COO, Agate Systems Ltd

"How refreshing it is to read a business book where the authors are not claiming to have discovered a new world-beating formula. *Humble Crumbles* is a 'warts and all' story of an entrepreneur and his business from birth to death, overlaid with an expert coaching lens. The style is very accessible, with section summaries called 'Crumbs of Wisdom' that are more like 'Wedges of Wisdom'. But the real beauty of this work is in the confidence the authors have not to make out that they are providing all the answers and, instead, to highlight the importance of asking powerful, pragmatic questions."

Alan Williams, Author; Founder and Managing Director, ServiceBrand Global

"*Humble Crumbles* is great. The blend of a real-life start-up story with practical business advice is a winning combination. I found myself nodding along (with a wry smile) at the tales, thinking how similar some of Paul O'Donnell's experiences were to my own, and loving the sage, yet simple, advice overlaid by Sylvana Caloni. If only this book was around 20 years ago!

Not only is this book concise, which is useful when you want clear direction, but the humour and experience shines through in the writing, making it an easy, fun read over a weekend with a coffee or two. Perfect for the busy entrepreneur who wants some help, but doesn't do dull!"

Nina Hampson, Co-Founder, Myla; Founder,
Zinc and Sideways Consulting; and Business Mentor

"*Humble Crumbles* offers practical and insightful advice that can only be gleaned from actual experience – the good, the bad and the ugly! Learning from author O'Donnell's first-hand knowledge of launching a business is so much more enjoyable and effective than simply reading about business concepts and the dos and don'ts of entrepreneurship. Authors O'Donnell and Caloni have brought together the powerful combination of real-life business success and failure with thoughtful self-reflection. *Humble Crumbles* is a treasure of a book for any aspiring entrepreneur."

Christine Brown-Quinn, Author of Amazon #1 Best Seller,
Unlock Your Career Success: Knowing the Unwritten Rules
Changes Everything

"Paul and Sylvana have created an engaging and highly valuable journey into entrepreneurship in *Humble Crumbles*. The book highlights two key skills that I have discovered in my exploration of effective leadership spanning four decades: the essential skill of paying attention to the right things, and the skill of effective judgement in navigating new territories. In *Humble Crumbles* Paul's story shows the challenges and pitfalls of these skills. Sylvana illuminates these and other crucial skills into focus points of 'crumbs' of effective action in this story of entrepreneurship that are not available in the mainstream narratives of the entrepreneur. A good read!"

Bob Dunham, Founder of the Institute for Generative Leadership; Co-Author of *The Innovator's Way*

HUMBLE
CRUMBLES

*Savouring the crumbs of wisdom from
the rise and fall of Humble Pie*

Paul O'Donnell and Sylvana Caloni

P
POWERHOUSE
— PUBLICATIONS —

Cover design and illustrations: Samsang Kelsang.

Powerhouse Publications
Suite 124, 94 London Road,
Oxford, UNITED KINGDOM
OX3 9FN

Dedication

*For Matt, Laura, Penny, Lulu, Chia, Eli and
Iva, who will create tomorrow's world.
And my co-author, Sylvana Caloni, for her
patience, creativity and insights.*
POD

*With gratitude to my many teachers and fellow
students in various communities of practice.
And my co-author, Paul O'Donnell, for his
courage, openness and capacity to learn.*
SC

Contents

Foreword

In my career as an educator I have found the most valuable classes and programmes are those where students gain experience in developing new ideas, get comfortable with intellectual risk-taking, and those that prepare them to engage the world with self-awareness and humility. Teaching creativity, innovation and entrepreneurship gives students the chance to develop skills and qualities that will prepare them for a range of future challenges and opportunities.

But, teaching creativity and innovation skills is not just valuable for college students and budding entrepreneurs – it can be useful for anyone, young and old. Today it is more essential than ever to equip people with the right attitudes, knowledge and skills to engage with the world successfully.

Starting a business can be daunting: writing a business plan; seeking the right kind of financing; reading the market; understanding legal structures; and the recruiting, management and personnel costs, among more. Learning how to build a profitable, scalable and successful start-up is indeed a challenge. And the learning around such a process is full of potential for real-world application – whether you are seeking to make a small change at home or work, as an intrepreneur seeking change within your organisation, or if you intend to change the world, or anything in between!

We know that confidence and real-world skills are crucial for anyone playing with new ideas or solving important problems, and the most effective way to learn is through real-life examples and stories. We all need to listen more to those who have been down the road before, especially when things did not go as planned. That is where the learning lies.

Paul and Sylvana have created an insightful handbook of the real-life journey of Humble Pie. They have constructed the perfect tutorial on starting a new enterprise, highlighting the hard work, challenges and the fun in a clear and cohesive read. I highly recommend this book to current and aspiring entrepreneurs, as well as those who are interested in understanding how to bring a new idea to life.

Elizabeth Hackett Robinson, Associate Dean,
Student Creativity, Engagement and Careers; Former
Co-Director, Centre for Social Entrepreneurship,
Middlebury College, Vermont, USA

Introduction

*"The time to repair the roof is
when the sun is shining"*
JF Kennedy

As a budding or early-stage entrepreneur, you just do not have the time to read a lengthy tome. Paul is a serial entrepreneur who transitioned from a highly successful career in global investment banking and Sylvana is a coach and former international equities analyst and fund manager. This unique combination of experiences and skills enables them to distil the major points of the Humble Pie[1] story for clarity and impact, focusing on key points that are applicable to all businesses and industries.

You may already have the ingredients for your new business. You know that you need an idea, proof of concept, business plan, contracts, staff and so on. However, these 'ingredients' alone do not make for success. Just like baking, too much salt and the pastry will be inedible; too high a temperature and it will burn; too low a temperature and it will not bake properly. Paul and Sylvana provide you with the wisdom behind these obvious ingredients and instructions. They peel back the layers of what may seem obvious at first.

Sylvana:

Paul and I came together to write this book to share his learnings and perspectives from his Humble Pie experience. In addition, I share my insights, observations and advice from my dual lenses as a professional coach partnering with executives and entrepreneurs, and as a former international equity fund manager.

We both mentor students at schools of entrepreneurship in London universities and facilitate Peer Advisory Circles for experienced and first-time entrepreneurs to help them make better decisions and improve their business performance.

We believe there are seven essential considerations that an entrepreneur has to embrace to generate long-term success:

1. Get a diversity of perspectives from an impartial sounding board, a coach and mentor.
2. Ask the right questions and really listen to the responses. Do not assume you already know the answers.
3. Troubleshoot: keep testing and checking in with your assumptions and plans.
4. Ask yourself, "What is my position?" and "What might be a flaw in my argument?"[2]
5. Know yourself and uncover your biases, blind spots and convictions.

6. Have a healthy respect for 'failure' as opposed to being defeated by it.
7. Have fun!

You may think that these considerations sound like 'motherhood' statements – vague, upbeat statements that give you the 'what' but not the 'how'. However, through Paul's story as the founder of Humble Pie and our insightful suggestions, we'll show you the how.

Paul:

Why listen to me? I founded Humble Pie, a food manufacturing and retail business based in London before the days of online delivery. Initially it was successful, but ultimately it failed. I set out to own the whole value chain; designing, producing and selling tempting and nourishing pies to an adoring and hungry public. My business failed because of that old chestnut: revenues were less than costs. Without a feasible prospect of reversing this situation, I could only sustain losses for a limited period of time.

My story is for real; the laughter, joy and exhilaration, and the blood, sweat and tears. I spent the first 27 years of my career in global investment banking. I rose through the ranks, travelled the world, and lived overseas, working in different businesses in Asia, Australia, America and the UK. I was an 'intrepreneur'[3] and loved every minute of it!

It also made me hungry to build businesses where I was the true owner – an entrepreneur. This is very different from being self-employed. Entrepreneurs need to draw on vast amounts of energy to build something bigger than themselves that will hopefully outlive them. My story and the lessons learned are relevant to you, whether you are someone with an idea, a graduate of a school of entrepreneurship, or an executive leaving the corporate world behind.

In the following chapters – we call them 'slices' – we capture some of the most important aspects of starting and successfully growing a business. You can enjoy the highlights, avoid some of the mistakes I made, and realise sooner rather than later that the core driver is really you!

This is not a technical manual or a textbook. It is about the equally if not more important human aspects of being an entrepreneur and navigating the complexities of creating, running and letting go of your business. The world goes on around you even though the 'biggest' thing in your life is the business you are about to create, which can impinge on your best-laid plans. In my case, within a few years my mother died (on my birthday!), the Global Financial Crisis impacted my core businesses, I moved house four times, and my wife and I went our separate ways. Real life mashes up with the workaday dramas that face any entrepreneur. But this is not a book about problems. Our goal is to provide some solutions, guidelines and helpful tips about how to more fully experience everything entrepreneurship has to offer.

How you read the book is up to you and the style that best suits your learning. It does not need to be read in sequential order. Pick and choose the topics most relevant to you or that you are most curious about; read it from the beginning to end; or, if you process information better by reading my narrative continuously, then read Sylvana's commentary separately.

We hope you find it illuminating and insightful so that you are better equipped to make a success of your dream.

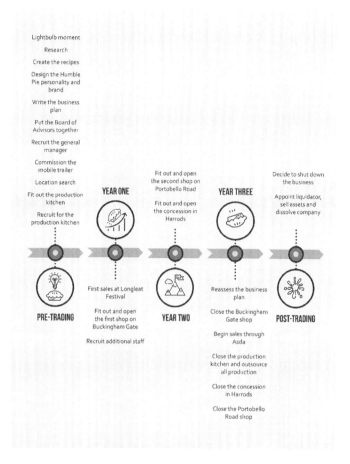

Figure 1: Timeline

Since Paul's narration of creating and folding Humble Pie is grouped by topic or idea rather than chronological order, we have included this timeline to provide an overview of how events unfolded, taking heed of the advice from scientist and philosopher Alfred Korzybski: "The map is not the territory."

SLICE 1:
Inspiration and catalyst

Just as perfecting a recipe requires experimenting with, for example, the combination and quantities of ingredients, the temperature and cooking time, so does perfecting how to be a successful entrepreneur.

Paul:

Context

I had such an overwhelming desire to be an entrepreneur! I wanted to enjoy the creative buzz I had felt when I was an intrepreneur working for large global banks. Only this time I would own a business that was not related to financial services and I would drive it based on my vision and values.

I had deep business and social connections with many people around the world. I was brimming with contacts whom I could call upon as sounding boards or potential clients. I knew financial services inside out and was very comfortable in this industry. So it is not surprising that my first forays as an entrepreneur were in adjacent businesses – financial advisory, financial publishing and two sales syndicates. My strategy was to create these businesses so that they were linked and designed to support and help each other grow. They generated reliable, recurrent income that was dependent on my Co-Founder and I delivering services every day. As a result of our successes, they also provided the capital to venture into unrelated business opportunities with different risks.

I was looking for a new challenge and to make something real and tangible, not just a service. I wanted to create a business that eventually wouldn't have to rely on my daily grind. It would be standalone and have a saleable value.

I was to find out there is a huge difference between having a passion or great idea and turning it into a reality that is sustainable and profitable. I was pumped up with great experiences, but I was to learn the hard way that much of this experience wasn't relevant or had to be greatly adapted to different businesses.

My entrepreneurial experience in creating and running Humble Pie was the best education anyone could ever hope for; the unexpected learning and challenging of my assumptions, beliefs and projections. I found that a combination of passion, perseverance, patience and resilience is critical for any entrepreneur. They keep you going when the tough times bite.

My lightbulb moment

I was on vacation in Sydney and feeling hungry when I stumbled across a pie shop. As I sat down outside to eat my lunch, I noticed a continuous stream of customers. What was interesting was that in the queue there were families, office workers in business suits, young people who had clearly just come from the beach, and workmen. In short, every conceivable category of person was lining up and patiently waiting to buy their lunch. "Why?" I asked myself.

When I finished my pie I realised why. It was delicious to the last crumb. I had never tasted a pie like it – and it was reasonably priced. I was drawn to the shop on another occasion and again noticed the steady stream of satisfied customers.

As a successful salesman I was fascinated to learn about how this business thrived. As an affable person, I was used to meeting people and enjoyed having conversations. I was good at asking questions and really listening, which put people at ease. So I didn't hesitate to ask the person behind the counter if I could meet the owner. The sales assistant disappeared into the back of the shop and a middle-aged lady emerged from behind the curtain.

Let's call her Mrs Horner. I explained that I lived in London and was curious about why she got into the pie business, her ideas, and her story. I made it clear to her that I wasn't a competitor who would steal her secrets.

She emphasised the quality of the pastry and the ingredients of the fillings. I was later to learn that the shop had a formidable reputation for its high quality, creative, savoury and sweet pies.

While England might have been the home of the pie, at that time this sector had missed out on the food revolution that had swept through the country in the late eighties. In fact, not a lot had changed in decades, dare I say, centuries, for the poor 'humble' pie found in many cafés, pubs or supermarkets. Generally, pies had a dodgy reputation for being dire, horrible, cheap, nasty, and unhealthy. This got me thinking about a market opportunity that was not being met.

My lightbulb moment. Maybe this was the idea I was looking for to diversify away from our financial services businesses? The healthy, nutritious and delicious pie! What an opportunity! What a gap in the market! By and large, Australian pies tasted great and had creative fillings. The pastry was a masterpiece of flavour and texture rather than a greasy or dry envelope to hold the insides together and allow easy transportation.

Now I was ready to get moving with some research and creative thinking that would help me form a plan to guide me on to the next steps.

Sylvana:

Start with questions

Paul's story demonstrates the hallmark of an entrepreneur – a sense of curiosity that enables them to see a gap in the market and ask, "Why not?" That gap may be a product or service that just does not exist. This provides an opportunity for invention. Or the product or service may exist, yet can be significantly improved or adapted, to meet the more specific requirements of subsegments of the market. Here there is an opportunity for innovation. Hence the idea of an entrepreneur as a disruptor of the status quo.

However, business success does not only rely on the market opportunity and 'what's out there'. It is also very much impacted by 'what's in here': <u>You</u>. As Abraham Lincoln said, "If I had six hours to chop down a tree, I'd spend the first four hours sharpening the axe."

Just as a business plan requires making assumptions and testing different scenarios, so too you need to examine what makes you tick. In your eagerness to get your idea off the ground have you taken the time to reflect and enquire to discover yourself?

Such self-knowledge may be dismissed as 'touchy-feely' by the hard-nosed business person, yet most businesses do not fail simply because of their product or service. The downfall of the business is often due to the unconscious, stubborn, desperate or hasty decisions of the owners or management teams.

Entrepreneurs are often very strong-willed and can be blinded by their passion and self-belief. Do not just assume you know what makes you tick. Make the effort to ask yourself the following questions and to reflect on the honest answers:

- What is my mindset and response to failure?
- What is my ability to adapt?
- What is my tolerance for risk?
- What is my ability to listen deeply?

Or better still, partner with a coach who can not only support you, but also hold you to account by holding up a mirror and shining a light on your unconscious behaviours and attitudes.

Motivations

There are many different motivations for starting a business. Understanding your drivers and fears will help to shape how you approach your business and its likelihood of success.

We cannot influence external factors such as economic conditions, legislative changes, customer preferences and the take-up of new technologies. We can, however, work on ourselves and how we respond to different opportunities and setbacks.

The 'why' or purpose

Being aware of what drives you will help you confront and overcome the inevitable bumps along the entrepreneurial road. It will help you persevere when a less-developed sense of why you are doing it might lead you to give up. It will help you stand firm and be able to respond convincingly when you receive the inevitable challenges from naysayers, be they family, friends, potential business partners or funders. It will also make it clearer for you when the obstacle is legitimate and a deal breaker and it is sensible to retreat rather than to persevere, simply to save face or pride. If you have not explored the 'why' of your business idea, then you can easily be steered off course by the many setbacks all entrepreneurs experience.

If your driver is to make money from a quick flip, then you will have less tolerance for taking the time to explore and have the necessary conversations with business partners, employees and other stakeholders. Or if your business is your hobby and a creative outlet from your day job, then you will not have the same commitment to making it sustainable in the long term. This is not my moral judgement; this is about making your business fit for purpose.

Crumbs of wisdom

- Prior experiences can be very useful. However, check if they are fit for the purpose of your new venture.

- You, the entrepreneur, will need to adapt and evolve with your business.

- Whether you are a kitchen-table entrepreneur, new graduate, or transitioning from a corporate career, do not assume you know yourself.

- Make a deliberate effort to take the time to reflect, enquire and discover yourself.

SLICE 2:
Preparation and sifting

Buoyed by the enthusiasm of their idea and what they believe is self-evident, some entrepreneurs will find any excuse to avoid spending hours preparing a plan that they think, in their heart of hearts, is just a waste of time. The problem is, without one, you not only have no roadmap to gauge the progress and milestones of your venture, you do not have a well-articulated and compelling story to engage potential investors and partners. Formulating a plan is not a waste of time because it is more likely to give you a better chance of getting the funding you need and will keep you focused on the path ahead.

Paul:

Exploring the idea

Remember Mrs Horner, the catalyst to my new business idea? Another interesting part of her story was that prior to taking on the pie shop she had never had any training in baking. In fact, she had won the business in a poker game and was completely self-taught!

I thought, "Of course, if she can do it, I can do it too." She was an inspirational role model and her story fuelled my curiosity. I took as many opportunities as I could to observe the customer dynamics of her business at different points of the day. I uncovered a number of important attributes of this business that weren't immediately obvious. Apart from a few breakfast customers and a few pies bought for take-home dinners, the vast majority of sales took place at lunch time in a two-hour window. The other thing I observed was that it was essentially a single-product business. No one really came in to buy a drink or a salad. They had to want a pie. It was a destination. Such insights were particularly relevant when I was putting together my business plan.

I heeded Mrs Horner's words on the importance of the quality of the pastry. We've all heard the saying 'necessity is the mother of invention', and this is particularly apt here. Armed with the insights I gained from our conversations, I returned home and started some desk research when I had some spare time from my financial advisory businesses. I knew that at this early stage I should still keep my 'day job'. I bought a copy of Harold McGee's food bible, *On Food and Cooking: The Science and Lore of the Kitchen*, and began my journey learning about the chemistry of food. The more I read and came to understand about baking, the more excited and convinced I became that I could make this business fly in the UK.

Testing the idea

I knew that if I was to go ahead with this idea, I had to figure out who was going to buy my healthy, nutritious and delicious pies. I couldn't afford Mintel market research, the go-to resource at that time. Nor could I afford a consultant to present me with demographics, consumer behaviour, competition and focus-group insights. So I continued with my own research until I eventually amassed enough knowledge to be dangerous. Despite my enthusiasm, I was realistic enough to know that no matter how good and thorough my analysis was, I would undoubtedly miss something. My hope was that it wouldn't be mission critical. In hindsight, I made sure – unconsciously – that my research would validate the result I was looking for. This would later prove to be an expensive mistake.

"Sounds about right," I can still hear myself muttering. I would discuss my ideas and findings with my Board of Advisors. It was 100 per cent supportive. Of course at this stage my Board of Advisors was just me! I was edging my way to creating a business plan. I did not need to convince anyone else, just me. I now have much greater appreciation of the importance of being aware of my biases and seeking impartial advice.

Translating the idea into a business plan

I did everything according to the book – researching, planning and budgeting. Tick, tick, tick. I built a fantastic business plan that I fell in love with. I had to really think through and articulate all the elements that collectively made up Humble Pie. People, places and things on one side of the ledger and resources on the other. This required patience and discipline. I had a ball putting together a storyboard of my Humble Pie in blazing colour.

My PowerPoint presentation and spreadsheets were elegant, had great graphics and showed clear profitable outcomes under various scenarios over three years – realistic, optimistic and pessimistic. Did I mention the graphics were spectacular? I also allowed some wiggle room to accommodate changes in circumstances and expectations. To me, the business plan for Humble Pie was well thought out.

However, when the rubber hit the road I discovered that while I had taken into account variables such as seasonality, I didn't take into account subtleties such as the opening hours in different locations. For instance, I would be paying rent on the shop for seven days on the famous tourist market of Portobello Road, but it would only make meaningful sales on two days when the market was actually open. Later, I realised that I underestimated costs and overestimated sales.

The problem at the outset was that I didn't share my business plan with people who were impartial, had different perspectives, and who could or would cast a critical eye over it. I shared it with my friends and, if they read it at all, they nodded in approval. This is a really important point. The people you share it with don't have to be prospective investors, they just have to be prepared to be critically honest and ask you some tough questions. I so wish I had opened up to them. In retrospect, I was determined to get Humble Pie up and running and I was not going to expose it (or me) to criticism that might take the wind out of its sails.

Anyone who was considering making an investment in the business wanted to understand what they were investing in and were keen to share my enthusiasm and passion. Articulating any plan is a sure-fire sign that it has been thought through and gives confidence to the person sitting across the table. It provides a basis for common understanding and establishing milestones. It really is not something overly academic that will be buried in the bottom drawer, never to see the light of day again.

Generally, no sensible and sophisticated investor will hold anyone to the letter of the plan. They will, however, hold you to mutually agreed milestones, share in the excitement when they are met, and definitely want to know why some were not met. While having a plan is no guarantee of success, not having one increases the chance of failure.

Communicating with your investors doesn't stop when you receive the funds, or your bi-annual review. It should be a continuous process where you are sharing good and not-so-good news. Don't shy away from conveying the bad news and asking for help or an opinion. It creates greater trust and may solve the challenge you are facing.

Coming up with ideas and assumptions for a business plan that *you* actually put together (not someone else) is essential. As a mentor to start-ups and students of entrepreneurialism, I am constantly amazed at the number of people I meet who have all the obvious ingredients for success except a plan. Creating your plan, testing it, and tracking how you are doing relative to the plan are all critical to its success. You must also get someone else who is qualified to review it for you.

Another cautionary note for your own business is that I built all my plans around the assumption that Humble Pie would be a great success. I had 'happy ears' – a term perfectly suited to overly optimistic salespeople.

I naively believed that if I spent too much time focusing on potential negatives or threats, I would not preserve my energy and would not do justice to the opportunity. But of course, leaving a sensible and well-thought-out exit strategy to the last minute is just plain dumb. Never be afraid to ask, "What if I'm wrong?" and "What is my Plan B?"

I did not have an exit plan, but I had a starting plan. It looked great and served its purpose even though it came with the shortcomings I inadvertently built into it.

Sylvana:

Pace yourself

Paul adopted a measured approach to starting his business. He did not rush headlong into it; he investigated his business idea while he was still generating earnings from his other ventures. Starting a business is stressful. Avoid adding to your stresses by prematurely turning off the tap to your current income stream.

As an entrepreneur you need to balance the tension of dreaming big and being realistic. Paul did not simply pay for expensive market research and consultancy. Initially, he made do with his available resources.

Also while you may not have the financial acumen or background to create your own business plan, as Paul advises, you need to go through all the inputs to that plan. As an entrepreneur your lifeblood is passion and conviction. In essence, you are sold on the idea. Yet you may be blind to critical factors or be overly optimistic. A good way to address this is to join a Peer Advisory Circle.[1] The members can test your assumptions, share their experiences, and provide impartial, non-judgemental advice.

More questions

As part of your ongoing quest to uncover any blind spots and get to know yourself better, here are some questions for reflection and action.

1. Why are you starting this business idea? Are you trying to prove something, and if so, to whom?

2. What are your values and vision? Spend time to work out what they are, honestly and thoroughly. They will act as your compass and determine what you will and will not do to transform your idea into a successful business.

3. Have you considered whom you can approach in your network? Can they recommend, for example, lawyers, accountants, or brand experts? How can they publicise your idea? Public relations firms really do open doors.

4. Are you too impatient? How do you pace your enthusiasm while maintaining enough of it to excite your potential investors? Many entrepreneurs who go to the wall have all their beautiful logos, branding, apps and expensive marketing materials without the substance of their business idea worked out.

5. Is there anyone within your network who has started a business? Have you sat down to speak to others about their experiences and the lessons they learned and the pitfalls you could avoid?

6. Who can you rely on for support when you start to doubt yourself? Have you explored membership of an impartial Peer Advisory Circle or found a business coach or mentor?

7. Do not just throw money at it. How can you 'test, learn and tweak'[2] your product or service? For example, have you established a social media following and created some excitement prior to going to market? Do you have the option to open a pop-up?

8. What are your deal breakers and how strong is your commitment to them? How do you know when you are being stubborn, as opposed to being 'ahead of your time'?

9. What would cause you to walk away from your idea? How do you guard against being in love with your solution and blind to its lack of viability?

Crumbs of wisdom

- Commit to creating a business plan. It is the basis for common understanding and establishes performance milestones.

- Share your plan with people who will be critically honest with you to avoid building in assumptions that simply validate the plan that you have fallen in love with.

- Be bold and upfront about delivering bad news or asking for help or an alternative opinion.

Remember Goldilocks' porridge had to be "Not too hot, not too cold, just right".

The real skill of a successful entrepreneur similarly requires balancing opposites.

You will need to balance the tensions of:

- Being a self-starter and knowing when to ask for help and advice.

- Your stubbornness with robust conviction. Do not be afraid to ask, "What if I'm wrong?" and "What is my plan B?"

- Reaching for the stars while having your feet planted firmly on the ground.

- Seeing possibility while maintaining sensible spending. Guard against 'happy ears'.

You will greatly increase your chances of success if you improve your emotional balance by being open, self-compassionate, experimenting, noticing your responses, and making small changes that build with practice.

SLICE 3:
Improvising the recipe

If a business plan is like the science of entrepreneurship, finding new opportunities, joining dots and making new connections is the art. Cultivating this art requires a mood of curiosity, lots of conversations, and being open to possibilities. In this slice we pull together the sources of many of those possibilities, including mentors and networks.

Paul:

Making connections

Early in my career I realised the wisdom of that old adage, "It's not what you know, it's who you know" that is important to success. By the way, I do not mean 'know' in the sense of being a great networker. (I hate that word!) I mean it in the sense of an authentic desire to know more about the other person and care about them. There is no doubt in my mind that it leads to ongoing success, sometimes at the cost of taking that little bit more time and effort.

It's not touchy-feely to have an interest in other people. It is a joy to be a connector and to generously share experiences and opinions. The side benefit is that you will do more business together over a longer period of time because it makes sense to both of you. Also, you make more allowances for each other because of the trust you have built, which will keep you going through the tough times.

As an entrepreneur I was always unconsciously filing away ideas, not discarding them. Opportunities arise in places that are not necessarily obvious. I keep my eyes open and can see connections that others can't. I enjoy meeting people and having conversations with no particular agenda in mind.

Finding a mentor

I was always on the hunt for inspiration, even at social occasions. At a weekend barbecue I met Martin Miller, founder of the eponymous gin. He was larger than life and a fascinating raconteur. I was intrigued by his stories and wanted to learn more about him. Like me, I sensed he was a very high-energy person, so I didn't hesitate to ask him to lunch. He was a serial entrepreneur, having failed and succeeded many times. He was a hotelier, photographer, property developer, publisher, artist, poet, author, antiques collector and gin maker. The list goes on. Remarkably, he left school at age 14. Just being in the same room as him changed the way I thought. He became my friend and mentor. He taught me and helped me realise anything is possible.

When you embark on an entrepreneurial adventure, the first thing you should do is find a mentor. If you don't, then forget about being an entrepreneur. It would be like building your corporate career without a coach. Discussing your plans with a mentor before you make the early moves is very smart. It helped me immeasurably. Having that 'outside-the-circle' trusted and non-judgemental person in my life kept me focused and, in some cases, gave me the courage I needed to make big decisions.

This person you choose, who accepts the challenge you are offering them, has a big responsibility. They offer a thoughtful view, another perspective that you can choose to accept, debate or reject. You may want to have conversations with several people. It is not just about their competency it is also about the chemistry between you. Additionally, ensure that your mentor does, in fact, challenge your assumptions. As I later learned, they need to be more than an inspiration or friend.

Being open to possibilities

If you are like me, you hate going to networking events where the game is to receive and thrust a stack of business cards into someone's hands while they look into the middle distance for the next target. It doesn't have to be like this, of course. More often than not, my most productive connections have come out of unexpected recommendations and referrals.

For example, surprisingly in a conversation with one of my contacts I learned that he knew a food chemist. Heeding Mrs Horner's advice – that the quality of the pastry was critical – I asked him to arrange a meeting for me. The food chemist made available a test kitchen so that we could spend a day to come up with the pastry recipe that I was looking for. For him, the attraction was that he would have a pretty good chance to get our business and for me I needed his professional knowledge. We succeeded and it was a win-win situation.

Another example of being open to possibilities came after I had launched Humble Pie and had three points of sale up and running. I was exploring how to further expand the distribution channels. To have my pies sold through a high-end, brand-name store was appealing. I figured we would benefit by association. The obvious difficulty with this strategy was how to get their attention. Coincidentally, I had been invited to the launch of an upmarket shoe brand. It was at this event that I was introduced to an ex-senior executive of the legendary London department store, Harrods. She was open to having a conversation and I had nothing to lose by being bold and asking her advice.

She said, "Just ring them up and tell the person who answers the phone that you want to speak to the Director of the Food Service division. They will put you through." So I did and they did put me through! Three months later

I was sitting across the desk from the Director, finalising details of my concession in Harrods' world-renowned Food Halls. I had assumed this would be impossible. The lesson for me was: do not assume, just ask. One conversation leads to another and opens the door to lots of possibilities.

Also, don't overlook the obvious – you need not go terribly far. Check in your own backyard! One of my network introduced me to a journalist who lived in my neighbourhood. She interviewed me for *Country Life* magazine, which was consistent with the higher-end brand personality of Humble Pie.

I was also very fortunate that the Public Relations consultant I had engaged was the son of Barry Humphries, the actor, writer and comedian. Barry very kindly penned a poem for us:

> *"I think that I could never spy*
> *a poem as lovely as a pie.*
> *A banquet in a single course,*
> *blushing with rich tomato sauce."*

We used this for some of our promotions and packaging. As my experience shows, time and time again it pays to be lateral in your thinking about how your network's network can help. You will be surprised.

As the plan came together and the business looked like becoming a reality, I had to understand exactly what I had brought to life. Humble Pie had a personality that reflected my ethics and values and the direction I was committed to pursuing.

Sylvana:

Managing your moods and emotions

As an entrepreneur, your principal role is to make your dream or vision real. It is easy to become dispirited as you get bogged down with the nitty-gritty of starting and running a business, so it is important to surround yourself with people and processes that keep up your spirits. Paul drew strength and inspiration from his mentor and the creative conversations he had with a broad array of people.

We've all seen those motivational posters or watched uplifting films like Kevin Costner's *Field of Dreams*, with its message of "If you build it, he will come." You might keep inspirational sayings in your wallet, your phone, on your noticeboard or on the fridge. You could read biographies of other entrepreneurs or listen to podcasts about how they overcame their challenges. Keep these front and centre to help you stay motivated when things get tough.

This is enjoyable and essential, not trivial. For all the talk of business as a rational decision-making process, your emotions and moods are critical to how you make your decisions and what keeps you going. Indeed, developments in neuroscience and biology have demonstrated that our emotions are intertwined with how we make decisions and, contrary to common perception, our bodies are not just the carriers of our brains.[1]

It will be particularly helpful for you to become more aware of your emotions and moods. In my ontological training, an emotion predisposes how we react. Another way of looking at it is as 'e-motion' – that which precedes a motion or action. For example, if I am angry, I might be moved to shout, punish, criticise or, in the extreme, strike something. If I'm joyful, I might be moved to smile, laugh, give praise, be creative, collaborative and assist others.

In a world that privileges 'rational thinking' and dismisses emotions as getting in the way of good decision-making, we tend not to develop much familiarity or understanding of our emotions. If you try to bury or bottle your emotions or feelings, you risk an explosion in which you vent like a pressure-relief valve on a boiler, or worse, you could damage your mental health.

I encourage my clients to build an awareness and vocabulary of their emotions by keeping a journal to notice and record their reactions to events. Some jot down notes on their smartphones on their journey to or from work. Others set up a spreadsheet and add to it in preparation for our meetings. Some buy a special notebook and set aside time to write down their observations and take stock of their week. Some share chapter and verse with me; others prefer to refer to their journal in our meetings.

There are several reasons for writing a journal. First, the information and experiences are yours. All the books on starting a business, entrepreneurship, leadership, presence, communication, negotiation and more will have limited effectiveness if you do not have a good appreciation of what makes you tick. Self-awareness is critical to self-management and relationships with others.

Furthermore, unless you record your experiences and reactions, you are likely to selectively forget – like that biscuit you had on your coffee break even though you're on a diet – or your memories may be embellished. Soon you will begin to see patterns and recognise your conditioned tendencies, and ultimately you will be able to distinguish how you respond in different circumstances.

Often my clients will make statements about themselves that they treat as universal instead of specific to a situation. They might say, "I get anxious if I have to speak in public." Yet if called upon to defend their children or something they care deeply about, they have no hesitation speaking publicly. In this example, distinguishing that in some circumstances they are not anxious or hesitant opens them to new possibilities. We can explore their emotions, what they care about, and how that emboldens them. We can then identify what they do well and 'map it across'[2] to another situation.

In time you will be better able to calibrate the success of the changes you are making. At first, when my clients modify their behaviour in response to what they have learned, they often overdo it. Like a pendulum, they swing from one side to another. It is with practice that they fine-tune the appropriate behaviour for the particular circumstances.

Eventually, you will see the progress you have made more clearly. This will give you the incentive to continue practising what you are learning. Be sure to acknowledge the importance of recognising your progress and take time to celebrate.

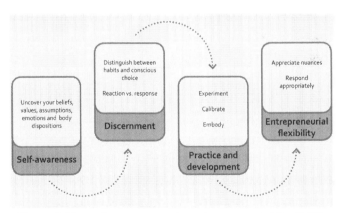

Figure 2: Four phases to sustain entrepreneurial flexibility

The first step towards becoming more self-aware is to notice, record and identify the patterns in your emotions, attitudes, behaviour and how you move your body. As your self-awareness grows, it enables you to become more discerning so that you can distinguish between habits – learned and often unconscious reactions – and responses, which are more grounded and thoughtful. Discernment allows you to choose your response rather than being held hostage to your habits.

As Viktor Frankl, the concentration camp survivor, author and neurologist, powerfully said: "Between stimulus and response there is a space. In that space is our power to choose our response. In our response lies our growth and our freedom."

Another reason for becoming more familiar with your emotions is that neuroscience has shown us that when we actively name an emotion, we activate that part of our brain that manages our executive thinking and allows us to respond more strategically. If we suppress our emotion, then we are operating from that part of our brain that makes us more likely to "fight, take flight, freeze or appease".[3] This is unlikely to lead to optimal decisions.

While emotions predispose us to behave a certain way in the moment, in the ontological framework, moods can be considered more as a way of being. We tend to face the world this way. Wearing both my economist and analyst hats, I've found it useful to consider a mood as a trend line and emotions as a curve around that trend.

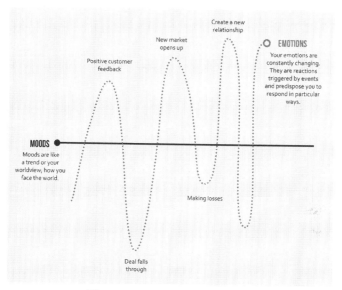

Figure 3: Moods and emotions

Let us consider some moods such as: acceptance, ambition, resentment and resignation.[4]

If I live in a mood of acceptance, then whatever happens I'm not likely to be rattled and I will just 'get on with it'. If I live in a mood of ambition, then what some might see as a negative event I see as an opportunity to find new solutions. If I live in a mood of resentment, I blame others or external factors and do not see opportunities. If I live in a mood of resignation, I believe I have no agency; that there is nothing I can do to make positive changes.

As an entrepreneur, you want to cultivate a mood of ambition. This does not mean you will eliminate negative circumstances and emotions – you will still have ups and downs, but you will not be floored by them.

Some years ago, I watched one of those 'secrets of the super rich' programmes, which focused on the experiences of Richard Block and David Quayle. They co-founded B&Q, the very successful British chain of do-it-yourself stores. After selling their stakes in the company, Block and Quayle, like many entrepreneurs, went on to create other businesses. At the time the programme was made, Quayle had generated even more wealth, despite having had some unsuccessful ventures. His response was to take full accountability, recognise his errors, and adapt his strategy. Quayle typified someone who lives in a mood of ambition.

In contrast, Block complained and blamed external factors for the failure of his business. He attributed the problem to the weak economy. He did not acknowledge his poor business decisions and did not learn from his mistakes. Block appeared to live more in a mood of resentment. This affected his resilience and ability to see new possibilities.

If you find yourself gravitating towards a mood of resentment, you can take active steps to shift towards a mood of acceptance. When we are resentful, we are often suppressing something. It may be hidden to us and will require us to explore our underlying beliefs. Do you believe you have been treated unjustly or unfairly by, for example, your business partners, funders, suppliers or customers? Are you holding back on having conversations that would clarify your expectations, different standards and what would satisfy you? Do you dwell in the past?

Aligned with a mood of ambition is a mood of curiosity. Walt Disney understood this. He called his research and development team the Imagineers. He realised that a mood of curiosity was critical to success.

Crumbs of wisdom

- Think laterally rather than assume. It all starts with an idea and a conversation that can lead to new connections and possibilities.

- Continually nurture and protect your relationships with mentors, investors and other connections – not just when you are short of funding.

- Cultivate a 'beginner's mind' – always be curious even if you have previous   experience in the field.

- Be open to saying "No." Develop this ability by becoming aware of your moods and emotions, and how you hold your body.

- Experiment with and practise shifting your emotions so that they enhance rather than impair your decision-making.

SLICE 4:
Kneading the ingredients

The obvious ingredients for the pie-making business are flour, water, salt, butter, meat, fruit and vegetables. The less obvious, but equally important ingredients, are the personality, values and ethics of the business, reflected through the brand and the products. Why bother? If you are striving to build a business that can stand alone and retains your DNA, then this slice matters.

Paul:

The compass: Personality, brand, values and ethics

A long time before I had produced my first pie or hired staff, I focussed on the brand I was building. I saw this as essential to differentiating our product and creating demand and loyal customers. I was very keen to have an authentic business I could be proud of. Pies had a very poor reputation because people believed that the ingredients were, frankly, rubbish. I wanted to create something wholesome, nutritious and profitable.

In fact, what I was actually doing was coming to understand and build the 'personality' of Humble Pie, under the watchful eye of our marketing guru, an ex-account manager at a global advertising agency, who was and remains a good friend.

You might think it odd that businesses and products have a personality. I thought that too when in conversation with the head of marketing at my former financial services firm. She often spoke to me in those terms. I just had not used those words or connected the dots. It had not been relevant to me, as it was someone else's responsibility. Now, as an early-stage entrepreneur with a completely different type of business, I realised it was most important that I devoted time to exploring and understanding this aspect of the business.

If you are transitioning from a senior corporate role to starting your own business, you will need to adjust your mindset and learn new skills. The shift from the corner office on the 25th floor with support services at your fingertips is stark. It can be lonely and scary.

These are some of the personality traits we identified for Humble Pie:

- Fun but not frivolous
- Genuine customer relationships
- Dependable
- Obsessive and passionate about quality
- Safe
- Family friendly

What I cared about the most was to create a product that reflected a set of values that meant people could confidently feed their families and friends knowing that the pies were good for them and had no hidden or nasty ingredients. These values were also consistent with offering an affordable premium product.

In parallel I needed to articulate the ethics and values that would guide our company. This was at a time when ethics and values were sometimes considered the 'soft' side of business. Many dismissed them as, "Nice to have, but what the heck? Are you going to make any money from them?" In today's world, where Impact Investing has gained traction, that is considered a dinosaur question.

What counts is the triple bottom line: people, planet and profit. The influence of social media means that if businesses do not behave appropriately, then their customers will express their dissatisfaction with their wallet and buy products and services elsewhere.

I knew more or less what I wanted. The marketing guy showed me how to step back from my own personal preferences and to consider those of our target market. It's too easy to think that if we like something, so will everyone else. Frequently it is this thinking that gives budding entrepreneurs the idea they are looking for to start a new business. This makes it doubly important to seek impartial or independent perspectives from advisors.

The marketing guy also taught me that there is a lot of psychology at play in people's reactions to goods and services. For example, drawing on my financial markets experience, I was very used to the colour blue being associated with reliability, trustworthiness and safety. On the contrary, he advised that there are certain colours that are not appropriate for the food industry. This was how we ended up with green, black and white in our logo.

He explained that marketing has to be based on much more than a hunch. If you don't know your product or service inside out, how can you expect to do anything with it? He walked me through a disciplined process that he had used successfully with major brands. After many creative conversations we settled on these values for Humble Pie:

- Transparency: What you see is what you get. There is no smoke and mirrors. It's very clear from our actions what Humble Pie is all about.

- Honesty: We often see taglines, particularly in the food industry, where terms such as 'good' and 'honest' are used. I believed it was worthwhile to stake a claim that our company could be trusted to do what it said on the packaging.

- Nutritious: Pies have had a chequered history, and at the time the general public associated them with poor quality. There were jokes around that no one knew what was in a pie. We wanted to set

Humble Pie apart from the pack. Our food had great and healthy ingredients that were not only good for you and your family, but were delicious.

- Creative: As a major point of differentiation, we adopted this value and delivered it in the form of non-traditional pie recipes. One of our mantras was, "If you can put it on a plate you can put it in a pie." We came up with recipes such as the breakfast pie, which had egg, bacon, black pudding, sausage and baked beans inside the pastry case. We had 40 fabulous recipes, most of which had no competition. (For your delectation I've included my three favourites, which were best sellers, in the Appendix.)

- Reliable: It did not matter whether our customers bought one of our pies from our Portobello Road or Buckingham Gate shops, our Harrods' concession or our mobile trailer at a festival. Our production was largely centralised to ensure consistency of quality and taste.

- Safe: Our production methods and staff training were designed to ensure there was no chance of contamination and that Humble Pie could be relied upon without hesitation.

- Friends and family: I wanted our food to be more than family-friendly and convenient. People would have no hesitation including Humble Pie in their family and social gatherings.

While compiling this list of values might seem like an obvious and easy task, once we got into it we recognised that we were forming the essence of the business and that it required considerable thought and analysis to get it right. The process also included establishing the look and feel of the pies themselves as well as their packaging design, selecting colours and fonts, and creating messages that would evoke a positive emotional response to attract our target market and retain its loyalty.

With the extensive research I had done, it was clear that there was an opportunity to fill the gap between the very cheap pies frequently found at sporting venues and the celebrity pies found in upmarket outlets. Our chosen pricing point was 'affordable premium'. While I would have loved to charge the high-end prices that celebrity chefs commanded, I knew that I did not have that brand equity. In any case I believed the middle market had more potential for us.

So far, so good. However, once your business has launched there may be consequences to adopting clear values and definitions for a product, which may come with expenses that you were not expecting. For example, we attempted to deliver a safe, reliable, nutritious family product using 100 per cent organic ingredients, only to find out that in some cases the cost of these ingredients was triple that of natural ingredients. (Natural in this context means naturally produced, minimally processed foods that do not contain manufactured ingredients such as introduced hormones, antibiotics, sweeteners, colourings, and flavourings.) After careful consideration I was satisfied that our values would not be compromised by introducing some natural ingredients.

This was a good example of having to rethink our approach to match the market realities. I wanted to stay true to the values we had adopted and recognised that entrepreneurs need to be nimble. You may find that your original idea is not economically viable, but you do not have to abandon it. You need to be pragmatic and determine what is non-negotiable and what is fit for purpose or good enough.

I cannot emphasise enough the importance of making the effort and spending the time to understand what your business is truly about. Too often I've encountered budding entrepreneurs dilute their great idea by trying to appeal to too many segments of the market and then creating confusing brand messaging. This could be easily overcome by devoting more time to this all-important aspect of your business.

Sylvana:
Differentiating between implicit and explicit values

Paul has discussed how he and his marketing guru worked together to develop the values and personality of the Humble Pie brand. This was not just a bolt-on exercise; it was intended to be the foundation on which he built his business. The brand values and personality acted *implicitly* as the guiding principles in decision-making and determined what was acceptable in the production, distribution and sale of the pies. They had consequences across the board in terms of how Paul operated the business, from the pies' ingredients and the suppliers used to the production methods, the design and colours of the logo and packaging, the type and location of the points of sale, and the customers they attracted.

To further reinforce and amplify how the values and personality that Paul identified impacted the business, the next step he could have taken would be to *explicitly* develop behaviour statements. Richard Barrett, the British author who writes about leadership, has spent more than 20 years exploring, publishing, teaching and consulting on values in personal and organisational contexts. He argues that there are two reasons for creating behaviour statements. First, they clarify what each value means in terms of day-to-day operations, and secondly, they provide a way to evaluate performance.[1]

You might be someone who is energised by idea generation and the chase. The actual execution may be less exciting to you or processes and manuals may make your eyes glaze over. However, do not underestimate the gap between intention and successful execution. From the perspective of your stakeholders it is much easier to be guided by a well-articulated written statement than to guess or make assumptions about what is in your head.

Working out these brand values and personality means much more than having colourful posters on your office wall. It means actually living them and translates into behaviours that are acceptable or not. This ensures consistency and reliability and builds trust and loyalty from business partners, advisors, employees and customers. Articulating your brand values and personality guards against shortcuts that compromise quality and create confusion.

As an entrepreneur you also need to spend time working out what your personal values are. Many of us neglect thinking about our values. We've learned them through our major tribes, such as our family, schools, religion and nationality. And you may be unconscious of your values because you take the view, "That's just who I am." A good starting point to determine your own personal values is to complete an assessment. You could do this by taking a free online survey at the Barrett Values Centre.[2]

Moving your values from unconscious to conscious is powerful. When we feel stuck, frustrated or demotivated it is often because our values are not aligned with those of the organisation where we are working or, in the entrepreneur's case, with the business they are creating.

A case in point, one of my clients was stuck. Let's call him Bill. He was a team leader and one of his team members, Joe, was not performing well. Joe was dragging the team down so much that they were not achieving their targets. Bill believed in the values of support and nurturing. He had had several conversations with Joe about how to improve his performance but they did not have any meaningful effect. On the face of it, letting Joe go conflicted with Bill's values. As Bill and I delved more deeply into what behaviours were appropriate and consistent with his values, he realised that by keeping Joe in that role he was not supporting and nurturing the wider team. His initial thoughts about how he should behave were too narrow. As he broadened his thinking, he was able to support and nurture his whole team and he moved Joe on to another role.

As Paul demonstrated when Humble Pie got off the ground and the costs of organic ingredients were prohibitive, he had to be nimble. He did not throw out his values completely. He adapted by purchasing some natural ingredients that were consistent.

Delving more deeply into your personal values as an entrepreneur

An illuminating exercise is to consider your top values. For example, let's look at the value of accountability, an important one for entrepreneurs, and some possible responses to it. See Figure 4 below. Then you can (i) explore your beliefs about an important value, (ii) how you behave to live that value, and (iii) how that behaviour might lead to unintended consequences.[3]

Value	My beliefs	How I behave	Unintended consequences
Accountability	I must take responsibility for my own actions.	When leading others I take on too much responsibility to ensure they do not make mistakes.	If others do not share my standards I am dismissive of their work.
	If I commit to a project, I must follow through at all costs.	I am very demanding of myself and others to complete projects.	Some find me intimidating and hesitate to share opposing views.
	I must not 'pass the buck' or blame someone else for my errors.	I take it on the chin, own up to my mistakes and apologise.	I am a perfectionist and excessively cautious.
	I deserve recognition and praise if something I do turns out well.	I am hurt if I do not get recognition for a job well done.	I withdraw and do not offer my creative suggestions.
	I must be on time for all appointments.	I am very disappointed when others treat appointments casually or cancel at the last minute.	I get stressed if running late.

Figure 4. Exploring your values. Adapted from the work of Richard Barrett.

Another positive result from moving your values from your unconscious to your conscious mind is that you will be more aware that they may be different from those of your stakeholders. You are then less likely to be dismissive of others and be more patient and understanding of their perspectives and behaviours. 'Walking a mile in their shoes' will enable you to have more creative conversations with less conflict and better outcomes.

Crumbs of wisdom

- Take the time to explore and define your own personality, values and ethics as well as those of your business.

- Go the next step to create behaviour statements that make the implicit explicit. These statements will act as the compass that will guide your actions and ensure consistency of your brand and marketing efforts.

- Market conditions and customer demands require you to be nimble. Values and ethics are not a straitjacket. With discernment you can make adjustments without compromising them.

- If you are feeling stuck, check in with your values.

- Separate your own preferences from those of your customers. It is not about you, although ironically you need to know yourself before you can let go and get to know the preferences of others.

SLICE 5:
The binding agents – relationships

As an entrepreneur seeking to grow a business, you need to move beyond your own capabilities and knowledge or you will become the bottleneck to expansion opportunities. This means that you need to create new relationships or rely on existing relationships from other settings.

Paul:

Choosing and managing your Co-Founders

Depending on the size of the market, the potential to scale up your business idea and its stage of development, you will have to move beyond being a 'solopreneur'. One way to handle this is to find a Co-Founder – ideally someone who is going to travel with you on the journey with as much passion and perhaps as much at stake as you. Choosing this person should not be taken lightly or on the run.

Many entrepreneurs believe that having a team to present to the world will enhance their credibility, particularly when pitching to potential investors. This is absolutely true and it's important to get the right mix in your team, whatever its size, to tell the story you want. Having one or two Co-Founders is important, but even more important is that you work and communicate in a complementary way and that you each bring skills that the others need.

Despite being one of the primary relationships in a business, Co-Founders' agreements are sometimes implied and unwritten because the individuals have worked together previously, are friends or relations. They often make the assumption that they have the same standards, expectations and vision, without having a frank conversation about defining their respective roles and responsibilities and capturing them in a written document. There have been several cases of high-profile Co-Founders falling out not only when their business was under duress, but even more notably when their business became a huge success (Facebook is but one example). I dedicated a lot of time, effort and money to have appropriate agreements in place upfront with my Humble Pie Co-Founder.

An additional and important action, if your Co-Founder is also your romantic partner, is that you set boundaries around your work and home lives. Just as in my own experience, I frequently witness Co-Founders being unable to switch off at the dinner table. They don't rest and recover from the demands of the business, which leads to negative consequences for their relationship and the business.

The importance of a Board of Advisors

In addition to choosing my mentor, I put my Board of Advisors together fairly early in the project. On reflection though, not early enough. I did recognise that the members' contribution would be valuable, but I was busy and felt I couldn't take the time to seek, interview and select each one of them. If I had to do it all over again, I would recognise that sometimes you have to take time, to make time.

As you might expect, initially I cast around the people I knew who I thought might be interested in getting involved. They were all friends – generous friends.

I wanted someone with skills in:

- Property
- Marketing and advertising
- Retail
- Law
- Accountancy

The marketing and advertising friend got involved very early. His contribution in helping me understand the personality, look and feel of Humble Pie was tremendously helpful. The others joined some 12 months later. The property advisor led an investment group and he helped me find suitable properties through introductions to estate agents. The retail advisor had decades of success and, at the time, had a warehouse and 23 shops in his livery. All of these people were very occupied with their own businesses, which of course meant that their time was limited. They weren't quite as on-call as I had hoped and, being first and foremost friends, they didn't really protect me from myself. In hindsight, what I needed were more people who would challenge me, offer alternative ways of solving a problem, and encourage me to step back.

While collectively the Advisors' involvement made a huge difference, where that difference diminished lay with me. I was so in love with Humble Pie that, one way or another, I was going to make it work. I would simply put even more energy into it and I would not accept defeat. Worse, eventually I became defensive and interpreted their advice as personal criticism and basically stopped listening.

What did not occur to me at the time was that Members of the Board and Advisors are not engaged for life. Better that they are involved at particular points in time when their skills are needed and most relevant. In other words, turn them over; engage them for an agreed term and renew their involvement at the end of that time if it makes sense for both of you.

Having a Board of Advisors sounds like something a big enterprise should be concerned about, not a start-up that is cash-strapped and little more than an idea. I disagree. If your ambition is to create a lasting enterprise, you need to be able to draw on others' experiences. I needed honest, impartial, knowledgeable advice.

Your arrangement with your Board of Advisors doesn't have to be overwhelmingly contractual. But you should work out some rules of engagement so you are all aware of each other's expectations.

Does it really make a difference? I did a lot of things right when building Humble Pie, and doing this was definitely one of them. I doubt the pies would have ever got out of the oven without them.

Appointing a Board of Directors

Whether your corporate structure is a partnership or a company, you are legally required to have partners or directors. They are the leadership team who manage and oversee the affairs of the business. These are important words. An enterprise is a legal entity and has its own life. The directors have a responsibility to protect and enhance that life. There is a tremendous body of law surrounding this and it's not to be taken lightly or seen as something that will get in the way of doing business.

Humble Pie was a private company and we had six Directors on the Board. I was the only Executive Director and some of the others were also on the Board of Advisors.

One Director was the representative of a significant outside shareholder. This is pretty common. It doesn't guarantee you will get a person who can really contribute. Rather, their job is to keep an eye on the boss's investment. You may have to agree to this as part of the funding deal.

Now what about the people who make up the Board? Here are some things to consider.

- Are they executive or non-executive?
- How many are there?
- Are they 'cheap labour'?
- What are their skills?
- Are they door-openers?
- Do they challenge or do they always say "Yes!"

In my case I didn't really need six, but I decided that their range of skills and experiences were important. I guess I should have listened to them more attentively. Perhaps I should have eaten some humble pie myself!

Negotiating with outside contractors and suppliers

Using outside contractors got me out of having to do everything all by myself. I realised very early on that I needed help with some critical knowledge and functional gaps from time to time and I didn't have the money to put all these people on the payroll. I used a combination of doing my homework and going with my gut.

The following are a few episodes where I could have done things differently. I needed an experienced food manufacturer that could potentially take over all our production and add to our wholesaling distribution efforts. At first I was cautious, as this was a key role. Having found what I thought was the right firm for us, we 'dated' for a while to trial them. Yeah! I thought I had found the answer to one of my biggest concerns. Unfortunately, a little more homework and I would have discovered they were having issues. To minimise the risk, I could have got references from their clients and the trade. Independent credit agencies and the Internet offer a wealth of relevant information and help to diminish the chance of you facing problems further down the road.

In one case, I didn't focus clearly enough on the terms and conditions. Not that I did not read the contracts thoroughly, it was more that I was too timid as a newbie in this sector. I did not know what questions to ask and I was too ready to accept what they offered me, deferring to their expertise. I could have asked my mentor or I could have run it by others in the industry to find out the generally accepted standard.

In another episode, I engaged a firm to do some financial modelling and market research for me. In our agreement we had specified a period of time and a monthly consulting fee. Where it came unstuck was that the work they presented was professional and detailed but not relevant to my needs. This could have easily been avoided by being more specific in the 'Statement of Works', including agreed milestones. We made these changes and the next piece of work they presented me with was very useful and insightful. The downside, of course, was that I had to pay for the work they had done prior to the restatement, effectively doubling my costs.

You will probably experience times when you are overwhelmed by detail and pressure to make decisions on the hop. For many, the solution is to simply push through and accept that at times you'll have to work 18 hours a day. This is not sustainable. Speak to your mentor to help you to stop, think, work out what's important and decide whether you really need to proceed this way or whether there are alternatives.

The highs and lows of recruitment

Employees not only make your vision or dream a reality, they also keep it alive.

Without exception, every person I have spoken to who either runs a business, owns a business or is a manager in a large enterprise is 100 per cent consistent in their view that the biggest positive about being in business is people, and the biggest negative about being in business is people.

As I looked more closely at my business and came to understand what I had, the complexity of my new world became increasingly evident. Although Humble Pie was in its infancy and I wasn't looking for many employees, I did need more than one. I started my recruitment search by placing an ad on Gumtree, thinking that this platform had broad and relevant reach.

At the time I was looking for our first general manager and some people to work in the shops and the production kitchen. I thought I would probably need about 10 people in total, and I was casting about to see who popped up.

I mentioned in Slice 4 that one of the mistakes I made was to assume I could apply, without modification, my management experience from my former bank job. I could have been more flexible when transitioning from a corporate mindset to that of a business owner or entrepreneur in a completely unrelated business.

I received 374 applications from as far away as South Korea. Many were seeking visa sponsorship; many had absolutely no relevant experience but argued their case well; and all had massive amounts of enthusiasm. I was determined to interview as many applicants as possible in the belief that I would learn all about them in 15-minute slots. I didn't have a baseline, so I figured this exercise would give me one.

I eventually did find the baseline I was looking for and I can't say it was a pretty picture. In many cases there was a gap between the written CV and the candidate's reality –

the embellishments to their relevant experience were creative, to say the least.

The result was a headache, but I learned a lot. It was a well-intentioned exercise that produced poor results and I never made that mistake again! Recruitment needs to be a considered process.

From then on, I found and used networks to refer people to me. I became much more focused and used some search firms. I also enlisted other people, whose judgement I trusted, to interview senior candidates.

In the end I did find my general manager, and she in turn found another 10 employees through her own network. I put a huge amount of trust in my general manager and employees and for the most part it was justified and paid off. It was impossible for me to handle all the minutiae that came with running Humble Pie and in any case I just didn't have the skills for some of the required jobs.

Over the life of Humble Pie, it had more than 1,000 items of equipment and ingredients, 50 principal suppliers, on average 35 employees, five landlords and more than a dozen service providers. At the same time, I was also responsible for three other unrelated businesses. Frankly, I was making a lot of it up as I went along.

I was also looking for some give and take from my employees and sometimes I was disappointed in them. I was prepared and willing to support my employees. I enrolled some of them on certification courses and other skills programmes. Some of them let me down because they pursued their own agendas, which were not necessarily consistent with mine. This probably says something about my naiveté. It did remind me of the difference between owners and employees, who do not have any 'skin in the game', nor do they want to. I offered equity to some of my senior people only to find that most were more interested in getting paid every Thursday and less interested in ownership. It just did not motivate them. It was another lesson in realising that not everyone had the same ambitions and motivations as my former banking colleagues and I had been used to.

Knowing how and when to delegate

As a consultant I've often noticed founders create problems when they treat their company as their baby and they are reluctant to devolve responsibility. This is a fairly common symptom of 'Founderitis'. Eventually an entrepreneur has to delegate and it should be embraced, not resisted.

In my case, as Humble Pie grew it became obvious I needed help. There was so much to think about and do, it was becoming overwhelming. My research led me to the conclusion that the best routes to market were a combination of a mobile trailer for festivals, retail shops, wholesale partners, and a concession in the fabled London department store, Harrods. With the production kitchen, I had five properties and numerous relationships to manage. All the properties were signed up, designed and fitted out, and up and running within two years from launch.

I thought this was a tremendous achievement and was proud of what I had accomplished in such a short time. I met the commitments I had made to my shareholders and myself in terms of building the business. However, in retrospect I think meeting all of these goals also sowed the seeds of our eventual demise. I moved too fast and was spinning too many plates. More on this in Slice 7.

It was my long-held belief that delegation was tricky, because delegation without trust was not only a waste of time but could also lead to a wrong (at best) or bad (more likely) result. I believed and operated on the basis that delegation was a gift and that trust had to be earned.

Since working with Sylvana, she has shown me the unintended consequences of this way of thinking. I suspect it came from having previously worked in a very competitive environment where the only person I really trusted was *me*. For Humble Pie, I delegated on a functional basis. There was a job and it had to be done. I generally did not trust, although I thought I did. I was not smart[1] about it.

Delegation didn't mean I could take my eye off the ball. So long as I could train properly, communicate clearly, and have the right processes in place it would work. For the most part it did. The idea of building and running a winning team was very attractive to me. Team success was my success.

Your relationship with the past

As I write, I am reflecting on one relationship that is frequently not recognised or given much space. This is the relationship with your past, and in particular, your past success. This is not to be dismissed. It is relevant no matter your background or stage in life. Sylvana and I facilitate workshops on 'Resilience: Bouncing back from Failure' for highly accomplished students of entrepreneurship. We address the difficulties in starting their businesses due to fear of failure. It can be particularly pronounced given their history of academic excellence and the high expectations of their family and friends.

In my case, my thinking and decision-making were very much influenced by a string of successes I had enjoyed throughout my career. This was not arrogance; rather it was misguided self-belief. Misguided because it was based on history and the presumption that history would repeat itself. "Past performance is not indicative of future performance" as the disclaimer on financial advertising often states. It would have been better for me to selectively apply all that I had learned throughout my career to my new business.

Sylvana:

You cannot do it alone

Make sure you have open and frank conversations with your potential Co-Founders and ask them why they are interested in the business idea and ensure that they know the risks involved.

Paul's relationships and interest in people allowed him to recognise that he needed external perspectives. He sought the assistance of his valued social circle and peer group; people who could guide and advise him at favourable rates. One of the benefits of taking the time to nurture and build trusted relationships is that it creates access to resources and capabilities you do not have on your own. A note of caution, however, is not to take your friends or family for granted. Do not assume that this is not a business transaction. You may have known your friends for a long time, but you still need to have explicit conversations about your respective expectations of what you require from each other. Too many 'mates' rates' and friendship agreements end in tears or, worse still, litigation, because the parties involved have not spent time to explore and articulate their assumptions and what success would actually look like to them.

Everything starts with an idea and the next step is a conversation. The Latin roots of the word 'conversation', are 'con' – together – and 'versare' – to turn over. So you might think of the conversation as, 'together we turn things over or make changes that achieve our objective'. Yet where so many of us have difficulty in conversation is that we do not stop to consider the other's perspective, background, beliefs, values, norms and standards. Too frequently we simply assume that our way of seeing and doing things is universal. This can lead to miscommunication, frustration, wasted time and the need for remediation, or making good.

This can all be avoided if we improve how we have conversations and engage with others. Whether you are talking to potential investors, engaging a consultant, hiring staff or attending a business briefing, you can prepare yourself so that you get the best return on the investment of your time and money.

Go forward with a fresh attitude and new approach, rather than, "I've been there, done that and got the T-shirt." Instead of treating the information as if you've seen it all before, look for what is different about the points made and the perspective the person has on the topic. In group conversations or team meetings, speak up, be prepared to share your experiences, and ask others about their experiences, interpretations and anecdotes. Even though you are the business owner, be bold in asking questions, no matter how seemingly obvious. Seeking clarity is something to be proud of, not ashamed of, and it is not a sign of ignorance or irrelevance. It is highly likely that you are articulating others' lack of clarity or what is unsaid by the team.

Pay attention to the quality of your listening. Be fully present, breathe, disconnect from the issues of your last meeting, and turn your smartphone off. Do not multi-task.

Manage your mood and be curious. Be open to new possibilities and be inquisitive about the speaker's perspective, the mood of the room and the stories shared by other participants in the meeting. Have compassion for yourself and others. This may sound touchy-feely, but it makes perfect business sense because it allows you and your colleagues to experiment, try things on for size, and consider each 'failure' as an experience that provides you with more information on how to adjust your strategy, approach and style.

Personal and business evolution

Different stages of company evolution require different skills and competencies. When I was a company analyst, I often observed entrepreneurs who were thrilled by idea generation, starting a company or making acquisitions, yet they lost focus and did not have patience or discipline when it came to building on those foundations, integrating an acquisition, and managing the 'business as usual' aspects of running a new venture.

In order to scale up, they needed to bring in people with the skills and competencies they lacked. In addition, just as their businesses were evolving so too they needed to evolve personally.

I cannot stress enough how critical self-awareness is to business success. LinkedIn Co-Founder and Chairman Reid Hoffman and entrepreneur and author Ben Casnocha draw a parallel between the continual evolution of companies and the individual. Their advice is relevant to you as an entrepreneur.[2]

Building on the questions we asked in Slice 1, I invite you to also consider:

- What energises me?
- What am I really good at?
- What drains me?
- What skills or competencies are a 'must have' versus a 'nice to have'?
- What skills and competencies would complement my strengths?

If you find these questions difficult to answer, ask those around you. Most people appreciate it when they are asked for their opinion or recommendations. You might be surprised to learn the qualities that they see in you that you cannot see yourself or do not readily acknowledge. Alternatively, you may overestimate how good you are at certain tasks.

Facing unintended consequences

Often we come unstuck when we have good intentions but our impact is unintentional or our execution is poor. One of my teachers, the late Judith E Glaser,[3] related an experience with one of her clients. Let's call her Mary. She had been promoted to CEO. She was a perfectionist who set very high standards for herself and her employees. Deep down she was feeling burdened by the breadth of her responsibilities. She feared they might not meet their targets.

Judith sat in on a meeting where Mary shared her vision for the company with her executive team. Judith observed that Mary became more overbearing and leaned over the board table as she emphatically presented her vision and what was required. In effect, Mary fell into what Judith called the 'Tell-Sell-Yell Syndrome'.[4] What Mary was unaware of was that her colleagues were physically withdrawing; they were intimidated by her and fearful to raise alternative points of view or objections to her vision.

Mary's intention was positive. She cared for her team and its success. Her execution, however, resulted in the exact opposite. Rather than building trust and rallying her troops to a common objective, they retreated and did not feel comfortable to share their insights, wisdom and creativity. Check in with yourself: How are you responding when your Co-Founder or team 'just don't get it'? Might you inadvertently be closing them down? Or, as Paul humbly acknowledged, are *you* closed down and only listening to what confirms your assumptions and vision?

Learning how to trust

If you are more comfortable being in control, then giving someone trust before he or she has earned it may sound risky. Yes, it *is* risky – and so is life! As an entrepreneur, you are continuously taking risks. It's a question of how risky and how you determine that risk. Just as you have to make assessments about financial risk, you also make assessments about people risks. Paradoxically the more you mistrust and control, the greater the likelihood of poor performance.

As your business grows, you cannot do it all on your own. You must delegate some responsibilities or functions to others. Delegation and trust are linked inextricably. You make it harder for yourself and take up more time if you operate from the belief that 'trust must be earned'. That is not to say that you should throw caution to the wind or trust blindly, however.

The leadership-development guru and author, Stephen MR Covey, created the 'Smart Trust Matrix'[5] whereby he distinguishes between four zones of trust. The sweet spot, or Smart Trust, is created when you place trust in others to do their job and validate it with evidence or due diligence. Contrary to some people's expectations, this is preferable to being overly wary which fosters a workplace where people do not feel engaged, loyal to management or give their best. Indeed, Covey provides examples where people are more likely to steal or cut corners and feel begrudging in such an environment.

Part of creating a culture of trust and getting the best from people is to demonstrate that it is safe for them to come to you if, and when, they make mistakes. You encourage them to be transparent and know that together you (or in a larger business, the person heading the project or division) will fix it. Instead of just talking about 'failing fast and often', show that you mean it and that you recognise it is part of the growth and development of your product or service.

Crumbs of wisdom

- Choosing a Co-Founder is an important decision and not to be taken lightly.

- Select people for your Board of Advisors who will challenge you, offer alternative ways to solve a problem and encourage you to step back.

- Remember that Members of the Board and advisors are not appointed for life.

- Take time to make time – do not skimp on due diligence and getting references and credit checks.

- Be explicit in your Agreements, Terms and Conditions and Statement of Works, based on frank conversations.

- "People are your greatest asset" may be an overused expression. Yet if you are to be more than a solopreneur and to successfully scale up your business, you need to recruit and manage people. This means getting to know your people and what they care about as well as their emotions and different communication and work styles.

- It takes time to listen to and understand the other person's drivers. Too often we assume we are all the same and we treat others as we want to be treated.

- Recognise that your previous experience and success in an unrelated industry may not apply to your new venture.

- Cultivate flexibility and a commitment to continuous improvement.

SLICE 6:
The folding of Humble Pie

*"No-one talks of entrepreneurship as survival, but
that is what it is and it nurtures creative thinking"*
Anita Roddick, Founder of The Body Shop

There was no single event that caused the crumbling of Humble Pie. It was more like death by a thousand cuts. Ultimately, the revenues did not cover costs. The strategy was revised in three stages: (i) outsource the production of the pies and shut down the production kitchen, (ii) close the concession and shops, and (iii) focus entirely on the wholesale route. Despite these changes, the financial performance did not justify remaining in business. Finally, all assets were liquidated to close down the company.

Paul:

Just before I tell the story about how I closed down my business, let's remind ourselves how exhilarating it felt to create and launch Humble Pie. That feeling lasts a long time and is an important part of the energy that kept me going. The downside was that this same energy masked reality.

I came to realise that the different distribution channels I pursued didn't generate enough sales for a cost base of four points of sale, a production plant and 35 staff. At the outset I was committed to investing in the business for up to three years, knowing that for most businesses it would take that long to start producing attractive results. After three years of trading it became clear that my original sales projections were overly ambitious and actual sales couldn't cover the cost base. Furthermore, I couldn't see where we would get the scale of traffic to make the retail shops profitable.

To make matters worse, the economy was looking dismal following the Global Financial Crisis. Our working capital demands were only being met in part from sales, so the only pocket left was mine. The source of working capital deployed came from my other businesses, which had also taken a hit from the Global Financial Crisis. So my options were limited.

Demand and supply

While my issue was that revenues didn't sustainably cover costs, yours could just as easily be being blindsided by robust demand. This may not sound logical, but if demand for your product is very strong it can be pretty forgiving of inefficiencies on the supply side. Additionally, because you think you are in a comfortable position, it may distract you from expanding your customer base, in the belief that there is no need.

For example, a fellow entrepreneur established a very successful marketing and advertising business that powered along for seven years. Then his biggest client, which represented 60 per cent of his revenue, went bust. He had worked hand and glove with that client – so much so, that it prevented his company from actively searching for and finding new clients and recruiting new talent to work with them. This had a negative effect on the valuation of the business when it was sold shortly thereafter. In his words, "It's a real problem, at that intermediate stage, when you are successful but not enough to expand your sales team without putting everything at risk."

In my own experience and discussions with colleagues, many new entrepreneurs have a dangerous focus on highly concentrated businesses that are too heavily reliant on a single or narrow customer base.

Taking stock and a radical change in strategy

My sales position and prospects prompted a major review of Humble Pie's business strategy. I needed to increase sales, reduce costs or a combination of both. I considered various options, ranging from tweaking our product offering and distribution channels to radically changing our approach. At this stage I was not yet contemplating exiting the business entirely.

One approach was to white-label the pies. That is, to anonymously produce the pies for another brand. I also considered exploring opportunities with the large supermarkets, in effect wholesaling.

The most effective way to reduce a significant chunk of costs was to shrink the business. This involved getting out of some of the points of sale, which reduced the headcount and operational costs.

You might wonder why I hadn't outsourced production of the pies at the outset instead of setting up our own production kitchen. At the time, it was a very expensive option to outsource, as the potential suppliers I had found required large committed volumes. Orders had to be placed six months in advance and, once confirmed, there was no flexibility to change the volume. Had I gone down this route, then I would have been hostage to the producer and overly exposed to their price changes. Even though I was very positive about the prospects for Humble Pie, I was prudent and wanted to retain control.

In the third year of trading, through my concerted efforts and using my connections, I eventually found another firm that was happy to take us on and be reasonably flexible on realistic terms. This enabled us to stop producing our own pies. We also extricated ourselves from the shops, the mobile trailer and the Harrods concession. This shift to wholesaling through supermarkets was a new experience and not without its issues. However, initially it brought good results.

It would have been great if I had been able to create Humble Pie as a marketing business from the outset. But, as mentioned previously, it wasn't possible given the circumstances at the time. From my experience, I suggest you consider whether you need to own the whole supply and distribution chain for your product. Given the advances in technology and the shift in market sophistication, today it's not only unnecessary, it's very inefficient unless you want to be a small-scale artisan business.

Exit strategies

The smart entrepreneur will have a Plan B or a parachute, just in case the twists and turns of running the business are not quite what was anticipated. I am very much a pragmatist. I react to the situation and solve it to the best of my ability and available resources at the time. In fact, I have a reputation as 'Mr Fixit' or the 'Go-To Guy'.

What I was not aware of was that I had fused my personal identity with Humble Pie. So I came to fear the potential failure of the company as a reflection on me. I did not want to be seen as a failure. So even though I could adjust on a day-to-day operational basis, I just would not let go when the writing was on the wall. I redoubled my efforts when deep down I probably knew I couldn't make it work. Sometimes this is referred to as 'flogging a dead horse' or a more sophisticated term is 'Plan Continuation Bias'.[1] In the end I had tried everything and I finally accepted that throwing more money at it was not the solution.

Getting out is at least as important as getting in. One thing is for sure: if you sell because you have to, you will probably get a bad deal. The key is, whatever outcome is in front of you, keep as much control of the proceedings as possible.

Most writing on this subject will speak of various exit strategies such as:

1. Selling to a competitor who is on a growth path through acquisition.
2. Selling to someone else who wants a relatively cheap way of getting into the space (very common in the pharmaceutical and tech worlds).
3. Closing the business completely and liquidating the assets as cleanly and as quickly as possible. It takes 15 minutes to create a company and a year to close it!
4. Being shut down by your creditors, who have lost patience and are happy to get 10 pence in the pound at best.

I decided on the third option. It was the least unpleasant and allowed me to retain a degree of control.

My accountants suggested a specialist company liquidator and the year-long process began. This is a legal procedure that has clearly defined steps. It is designed to protect all parties and, from my experience, I think it works well. The point is, you have no say in proceedings. However, I did retain some control as it was a voluntary wind-up. It was straightforward, particularly as it did not result from the actions of creditors. Nevertheless, it was bewildering and overwhelming. The standard form you must complete in these circumstances makes you feel like a total loser.

Additionally, I was surprised to find the emergence of personal guarantees that I had forgotten about. These covered the accountant's fees, rent, bank overdraft and equipment leases. I had mistakenly thought they would be covered by the liquidation. Not so. They were effectively secured creditors secured by me personally.

The lesson I learned is, *read every document that you sign*. For the most part I was diligent. But sometimes I got caught up in the euphoria of getting my business off the ground, or I was exhausted and did not spend enough time going through the fine print. I just believed everything would be okay in the end.

One of the most difficult aspects of this experience was having to acknowledge that Humble Pie had failed, and having to bear the brunt of most of this alone.

The point I'm making is that at this stage of proceedings, if a business fails, there are some unexpected consequences. People lose their jobs. I lost my job. The company's debts do not just vanish into the liquidator's ether – some come home to roost.

The time it took to shut everything down was exhausting and something I hadn't planned for. It is not a matter of just walking away from it all. Guided by my values and ethics, that was something I was unable to do. The other great difficulty was informing the shareholders, my wife and family. This was very painful for me. When I was feeling low, I was touched by a number of emails I received from shareholders, thanking me for the great work I had done and my tremendous effort trying to make Humble Pie work.

The recovering entrepreneur

It took me some time to rebuild my confidence and energy, let alone my financial health. During this time, I also discovered some things about myself that I had not focused on or did not realise before. My business ethics survived intact and I really cannot do everything. But I can actually do quite a lot!

I think I was too proud to fail. I had a version of Founderitis and could have wound up Humble Pie earlier. I also didn't have a sustainable work-life balance! I was working every hour of the day, every day, and this impaired my clarity and the quality of my decision-making. I had forgotten that sometimes it is just time to move on. Sometimes it becomes clear there are better ways to spend your time. I underestimated the amount of physical and emotional energy I needed to get through this. Not to put too fine a point on it, 80 per cent of small businesses fail within the first five years, so I had plenty of company.

I had never realised the cost of getting out was at least as much as the cost of getting in, took far longer and was more stressful. The lesson I learned the hard way is to plan your exit with as much diligence and attention to detail as your entry.

It was clear our exit price was close to zero as the present value of future sales was very poor. All that could be sold was some second-hand equipment. Humble Pie is a great brand name and I did not have the resources to exploit it properly. It was an Academy Award winner and a box-office flop.

Sylvana:

Identity and mindsets

An important takeaway from Paul's experience with Humble Pie is that the entrepreneurial spirit is about adaptability. You start with a skeleton, you flesh it out with your business plan, and then 'life happens'.

Paul reveals that he had fused the identity of Humble Pie with his own identity. He believed that if the company failed it would be *he* who failed. In many ways this is unsurprising and understandable because, like most entrepreneurs, he lived and breathed the business. This gave him the energy to push on, to relentlessly try to find solutions to make it work. The downside of this fusion of identities is, as he acknowledges, that his energy masked the severity of the deteriorating conditions. This fusion probably contributed to Paul's defensiveness, which meant that sometimes he would dismiss the suggestions his advisors made because it would conflict with his positive energy and he feared it would prevent him from pushing forward. Had he been able to disassociate himself more from Humble Pie, it is likely that he would have let go earlier.

Another way to look at this is to consider the work of psychologist Dr Carol S Dweck, who coined the terms 'fixed' and 'growth' mindsets.[2] She explores people's way of thinking and how this impacts on their behaviour across sectors including sports, business and entertainment. She concludes that those who have a growth mindset are more likely to succeed over time. Where they fail, they take it on the chin. Their view is, "My strategy or the way I did it is what failed. I am not personally a failure." So they are better able to step back, look at the situation objectively and determine how they can adapt the way they do things to create success next time round. They behave as if they are not there yet, rather than thinking they'll never get there.

In my interpretation of the fixed mindset, the individual's identity is so wrapped up with what they do, or their business, that when it fails they attribute the failure to themselves (their talent and intelligence) rather than to how they are running the business. Hence they are less likely to rebound quickly and consider how they can adapt their strategy to succeed next time.

If your response is, "Nice theory, but that's just who I am" this may be a clue to your fixed mindset. The good news is that our brains have what is called 'neuroplasticity' and so, with intentionally noticing, becoming aware, and unlearning old ways of thinking and doing things, we can learn new ways of thinking and doing things to shift to a growth mindset. To illustrate this point with a road map, return to Figure 2 'Four phases to sustain entrepreneurial flexibility' in Slice 3.

Some ideas to reflect upon that you might find illuminating are to:

- Notice when you say, "That's just who I am" or "It's in my DNA".
- Consider what you could do differently if you reframed "That's who I am" to "That's the way I've always done it" and even more powerfully, "I can learn to do it differently".

- Examine your attachment to your self-identity. When does it work for you and when does it add to your burdens?

For all the talk of 'overnight success' and the excitement about unicorn stocks, consider that even very successful, internationally known entrepreneurs have a number of business ideas that did not get off the ground. And, even if they are up and running, some way down the line they may recognise that their initial assumptions cannot be realised. A number of factors may be at play. Conditions may change, new technologies might open up new possibilities, customers may respond differently and the entrepreneur has to repurpose their initial ideas and pivot the businesses on the road to ultimate success.

In their book, *The Start-Up of You*, Hoffman and Casnocha provide scores of examples of companies that have become household names and part of our daily life, but which evolved differently from their founders' initial concept and plan. For example, did you know that Netflix was not successful in its original formulation?[3]

Setting boundaries

You might be thinking, "I work flat out, every single day of the week, when do I get the time to take a breather, watch a film, read a book, listen to a podcast, reflect on questions and write a journal?" People who are overwhelmed often do not set boundaries on their time.

They overcommit as they are not used to saying "No" and their default position is to accept a task or obligation. This may be because they have a self-belief that they are never enough, and/or they are used to pleasing others or taking on excessive responsibility.

It may also be that they do not have the body to say "No". You might be wondering what your body has to do with anything. Let me illustrate with the example of some of my clients. One was really creative, constantly coming up with new ideas and product developments and, like Paul, could see connections and opportunities where others could not. My client was enthusiastic and excitable; a bit like a 'happy puppy'. By contrast, his boss was cautious, would not give approval without a budget code and at the office was known as "Dr No".

Needless to say, they were often at loggerheads. The happy puppy did not like the tension that he felt in his body when he logically knew he had to say "No". He quelled the discomfort by saying "Yes". Dr No, on the other hand, had become rigid over time. He quelled the discomfort in his body that arose from not being in control if he said "Yes".

As I coached them, each became more aware of how his body was reacting, where the discomfort was situated, and how he habitually took action to quell the discomfort in his body. Each practised different ways of standing, moving and sitting to become more flexible and to be able to make choices about how to respond rather than react from habit.[4]

Some people overwork because they are drained and it takes them longer to complete tasks or they have to correct their mistakes. They push through and ignore the messages that their body is sending them – for example, tight shoulders, a sore lower back, headaches or itchy eyes. In its extreme, when you ignore such signals, your body takes over and you can become seriously ill or suffer from mental health issues. Taking a breather, getting up and stretching, walking around the block, staying hydrated and chatting with someone can re-energise you. By taking time out you actually 'make' time because you will be more creative and efficient when you are rested and in a mood of curiosity.

Some people become overwhelmed because they are reluctant to delegate 'their baby'. They want everything done to their high standards. They have not learned the distinction between perfection and 'good enough' or 'fit for purpose'. Pardon the pun, but this does not mean throwing the baby out with the bath water or adopting sloppy standards. It means being more thoughtful about prioritising and determining when and what has to be done to the highest standards and what can be done at a lower *and* sufficient standard for the purpose.

Navigating overwhelm

If you are feeling overwhelmed, you will not make the best decisions for your business. As we've seen, you may become overwhelmed because you agree to too many commitments, tasks or responsibilities. You do this as a way to ease the discomfort in your body, which is not accustomed to setting boundaries. Or you may not be practised at making declarations, such as saying "No", or being explicit about what meets your requirements.

Performance consultant Robert Dunham's work on how leaders and executives overcommit and become overwhelmed is equally applicable to entrepreneurs. Dunham points out that many of us fill our diaries with commitments that are impossible to fulfil given our capacity. He argues:

> *"Managing capacity is a skill. You can learn and improve this skill over time. Managing capacity is a practice, in which you must engage continually to be an effective leader, executive or manager [or entrepreneur]."⁵*

He identifies seven stories that we tell ourselves, which lead to or maintain our overcommitment. For our purposes we'll focus on just a few of these. We may simply be blind to it until something breaks down or our customers complain. Here we are considering customers in a broader context. That is, they are stakeholders and could be buyers, colleagues, shareholders, the investment community, suppliers or your family and friends.

You may play the hero or heroine. That is, you believe that it is your responsibility to do more. You see this as part of being the best and you attribute your success to going the extra mile, taking additional time, and working long hours and weekends. You may recognise that you are overcommitted but you are hopeful. Your thinking is, "I'm not sure I can pull this off and I believe good things happen to good people so it will work out in the end."

You may be in resignation, where you feel you cannot avoid overcommitting and that you are unable to tell your customers that you will not be able to deliver on time or to specification.

Do any of these stories sound familiar to you? If you find yourself continuously overwhelmed, then for the sake of your health, creativity, quality of decision-making and good customer (stakeholder) relationships you first need to accept that you are not superhuman and you need to take stock of how you are spending your time. Dunham recommends setting up a worksheet where you enter your commitments and a reasoned estimate of the time it will take to complete them at an acceptable standard. Once you've made this analysis you will probably find that you have committed to many more hours than you have available and you just do not have the capacity.

A common fear is that if you say "No" you will lose potential business or damage your customer relationships. On the contrary, if you say "Yes" and repeatedly fail to deliver, you will damage your reputation for trustworthiness with your stakeholders.

If your capacity is fixed in the short-term, Dunham recommends several actions you can take and conversations you can have with your customers to take care of them and safeguard your longer-term relationship.

Too often customers are left hanging in the air by vague commitments. This causes frustration and disruption for your client, especially if your product or service is a component of their business. It is better to decline the order by stating upfront that you are overcommitted. Or you can revoke an order and manage the consequences for the customer, giving them notice so they can make alternative arrangements. You can transfer the order to another firm. I can hear some of you saying, "Are you mad? I'd never give a job to a competitor!"

What is most important is not the short-term deal. It is the long-term relationship and trust you build with your clients. If they feel that you have their best interests at heart, they will appreciate your gesture and work around it and come back to you for future orders. If you repeatedly disappoint, you will get a poor reputation and lose your customer forever.

You could delegate the task to someone else within your team. Or you can make a counter-offer. This would involve having an honest conversation with your customer about what would be acceptable to them given your limited capacity. Consider this a dynamic re-specification of the order. Or, similarly, you could clarify priorities to determine if any part of the order could be deferred or not completed.

Crumbs of wisdom

- Take the time to read the full contract or ensure that you have a lawyer to point out the Terms and Conditions.

- As much as your business is your baby, you need to maintain a healthy distance from it so that you do not fuse your identity with it.

- Check in with advisors to guard against Plan Continuation Bias.

- Explore how you respond to failure, whether you have a fixed or growth mindset and cultivate adaptability.

- Become aware of your moods and emotions to maintain your physical and mental health and to make better decisions.

- To manage your capacity, evaluate the commitments you make and learn strategies to avoid overwhelm.

- Expand the range of how you hold and move your body so that you are not always rigid or always flexible and can manage overwhelm and overcommitment.

SLICE 7:
The benefits of hindsight

If, like many entrepreneurs, you are thinking that your situation is unique, you might be surprised to know that your experiences are shared by many. From the story of the rise and fall of Humble Pie, you can take the insights that are relevant to you. Most entrepreneurs become exhausted and are blindsided by their fears and passion. They are often too close to the business. This can mask the creep of poor decisions. On their own, poor decisions may not be dangerous but as they accumulate they can become fatal. And, of course, there will be some insights that we've shared that you will need to adapt to suit your specific circumstances and business.

Paul:

The whole purpose of telling you my story is to identify some of the thinking and behaviours that produced successful results. And, more importantly, to expose the ultimately negative thinking and behaviours that were not evident to me at the time. This lack of awareness created a mismatch between what I intended to do, how I did it and the way it turned out. I now recognise I could have done things differently to achieve better results. I've also since learned how to do them differently.

In essence, the demise of Humble Pie was partly due to external factors that I could not control. For example, we were hit by massive increases in the costs of key ingredients, such as dairy, when demand from the Chinese market exploded. We were unable to pass on these cost increases to the customer. This was coupled with a deterioration in the UK economy negatively impacting consumer behaviour. It was also partly due to factors that I *could* control.

Although I made many good decisions, I certainly made some duds. I let what was going on around me get the better of me and this affected my decision-making. On reflection, there were seven major factors that impaired the quality of some of my decisions. They did not all happen at once, of course, but they did seem to become more prevalent over time, as I succumbed to the pressures of running a very demanding business.

A useful way to guard against this happening to you is to think of yourself as an athlete. Being physically and mentally prepared is the starting point, but you need to keep up the momentum. It's worth looking at the seven factors that had a negative impact on me in more detail.

1. Multi-tasking and splintered focus

At the time, conventional wisdom was that multi-tasking was necessary if you wanted to be successful. I certainly bought into this as a badge of honour. However, I learned the hard way that multi-tasking absolutely does not work for complex situations. All you achieve is to work far too hard, only to experience stress and fatigue and be faced with lots of half-finished tasks. It's not smart. Sequential tasking and delegating gets everything done properly. This requires trust and letting go of your baby.

2. Spinning plates

I had too many unrelated projects and situations on the go simultaneously. At the time I launched Humble Pie, I was also the Co-Founder and COO of three other unrelated businesses and had established two international marketing and sales networks. With my high energy levels and can-do attitude, I believed anything was possible with ever more hard work. However, this was a fallacy. I was 'chief cook and bottle washer' and at times I was so drained I felt like I was on a roller coaster. As a result, I did not make the best decisions.

3. More haste, less speed

I was propelled by the need to do things quickly; to prove something and to keep the commitments that I had made to my investors and myself, without realising I could have renegotiated or adapted these commitments, contracts with suppliers and my business relationships. I didn't work through some options that were available to me because I thought that I had to have an immediate answer to an issue or challenge. By taking more time I would not have made decisions on the hop or out of desperation. Sometimes you need to take time to make time.

4. Not independently testing the idea

I was so excited and convinced by my idea that I didn't put enough effort into independent, targeted market research and focus groups. I did a lot of my own research, such as watching the traffic in and out of Mrs Horner's shop at different times of the day, having conversations with experts and reading relevant material. I also got an early idea of the customer response to our pies through the mobile trailer that we used at festivals. For a deeper understanding of potential customer demand, I should also have set up focus groups. Also, it would have been better to trial points of sale in regional centres, where the costs were much lower than central London, before I took on long-term leases and capital expenditure.

5. The wrong tools for the job

I went into Humble Pie with the instincts and knowledge I had accumulated from my previous employment and other businesses. Some of these turned out to be the wrong instincts and knowledge for the retail food business. I had enormous enthusiasm, huge energy and great passion. I already had many of the right skills to run a business in general. I knew how to do accounting. I knew how to do spreadsheets. I knew how to negotiate and how to run successful teams of like-minded, similarly driven peers who aspired to leadership. I knew how to work all the hours that God sent me. These were not enough to compensate for my lack of knowledge of the idiosyncrasies of a retail food business.

6. Neglecting my work-life balance

Running a business from the get-go is a very isolating process. Just as an athlete has to draw on energy from within, so too does an entrepreneur. Not to stretch the sporting analogy too far, but entrepreneurs have to take care of themselves to reach and maintain peak performance. For me, one of the best ways to maintain my energy was meditation. I was fortunate to learn this practice when I was working at the bank, many years before, so I came into Humble Pie armed with its benefits. The clarity of mind I achieved was invaluable. It did not require me to wear Lycra (not a good look) and could be performed in any quiet space. With all the demands on me, it was too easy to let this practice slip. In any case meditation alone is not enough.

In addition to my mental wellbeing I also needed to make sure that I was doing some exercise and eating properly.

This sounds obvious, but I was not good at the former, although I was very aware of it. It's also smart to re-energise by having a completely unrelated hobby. You may not know that Winston Churchill's hobbies were brick laying and painting. He firmly believed, as I do, that if you do not have balance in your life your thinking will be unbalanced.

7. Selective deafness

I went through the motions of seeking independent perspectives and challenges to my plans by finding a mentor, creating a Board of Advisors and getting expert advice. But if I'm really honest, I only half-listened because I was so convinced my plan would work. Humble Pie had become a part of my identity. Blind determination is exactly that. It makes you blind.

My story is intended to alert you to the issues that new entrepreneurs encounter before they become problems. It provides a checklist that might improve your chances of success. It is a catalyst to change your thinking, your approach to risk and your decision-making.

Cheers! And I hope you enjoy making and eating the pies.

"Failure is the condiment that gives success its flavour"
Truman Capote

 **Sylvana:**

As Paul's experience shows, it is not possible to sustain overwhelming hours and responsibilities for an extended period. Of course, there are times when you'll have to burn the candle at both ends to meet a deadline, but you cannot make that a habit. You must take care of your physical and mental wellbeing; let go and bring in additional technical competencies and skills. Take breaks, play with your kids, get out into nature and spend some downtime on creative interests such as music, art and photography to exercise another part of your brain's neural networks.

If you believe your success to date results from being your own person and doing it alone, follow the example of high-performance athletes who build a team around them that includes, for example, physical therapists, nutritionists and coaches to improve and sustain their performance. I urge you to reframe your thinking if you consider this type of assistance and support as 'weakness'.

In the following table, I've summarised the insights gained from peeling back the layers of Paul's thinking and actions. I have put it together as a reference tool for you to explore at different stages of your business development.

Many of the steps Paul took are the common advice you'll find in business courses and books on entrepreneurship.

Where he came unstuck was going through the motions of such advice without having an understanding of what was really motivating him. What his reflections and deeper analysis illuminate is that without having a good understanding of your drivers, assumptions, values and fears you run the risk of inadvertently setting yourself up to fail. As the old adage goes, "Forewarned is forearmed".

Summary of actions and insights

Action	Insight
Create a business plan	The usual drill is to create three scenarios – positive, neutral and negative.
	Be aware that you might have self-fulfilling assumptions or that you could be unconsciously biased in support of your product or service so that even your 'negative' scenario is unduly positive.
	Seek impartial perspectives and be open to your assumptions being challenged.
	Ask, "What is my position?" and "What might be a flaw in my argument?"
	Check if you are being defensive and treating your idea like your baby.
Test, track, learn and adapt 'Fail fast, fail often'	You cannot be an entrepreneur if you are not passionate about your idea and convinced of its success.
	However, you need to test your idea and get different perspectives and reactions.
	Consider a Peer Advisory Circle, focus groups, low-cost markets or pop-ups before you commit long-term capital to fixed assets.
	Be realistic about how much time you give your idea. Entrepreneurs can be stubborn and not want to give up because they do not want to be considered a failure.
	Stay alert to 'Plan Continuation Bias'.

Action	Insight
Actively create and rely on your network	There are too many networking events where people thrust a business card at you, put you on their distribution list or look beyond you to the next 'sales target'.
Connectors and mentors	Take time to listen and create genuine relationships. Ask questions and do not assume that each of you has the same understanding or expectations. Check in, find out what works best for them, and share what works best for you.
	When seeking a mentor recognise that different people may be appropriate at different stages of your business plan.
	Being an entrepreneur can be lonely. An encouraging and inspirational mentor can be very supportive. Make sure they are also able to challenge your thinking.
	Instead of just looking for people who have succeeded, look for people who have failed, learned from their experiences and reinvented themselves and their business.
	Cultivate a mood of curiosity. Some of the best connections come from unexpected places, people and ideas. The path to success is not a straight line. If you mix with the same people, you'll get the same perspective and ideas.
Brand, Personality, Ethics and Values (BPEV)	These are not just buzzwords that you palm off to a communications expert.
	As the entrepreneur, you need to be actively involved in creating the brand, personality,

Action	Insight
	ethics and values of your business. They will impact how you conduct your business and how you engage with your employees, customers and suppliers.
	Whether you are in it for a 'quick flip' or the long haul, BPEV is your compass in the tough times.
	If you've come from a corporate background or another type of business, check in with yourself that your assumptions are relevant and applicable to your new business, context and economic environment.
Co-Founders	So-called 'self-made' entrepreneurs do not do it alone. They have advisors whether they acknowledge them or not.
Board of Advisors	Create a Board of Advisors early in the process and listen to what they advise. You may not adopt their perspectives, but be open to considering their advice and comprehensively thinking it through. It could save you from persisting in a strategy that is not likely to succeed because you are inexperienced, unaware or blind to unexpected factors.
	Early course-correction can save you a lot of time, frustration and money.
	You may start out with friends as Co-Founders or advisors. Be careful that they are not just cheerleaders and afraid of ruining your friendship by challenging you.

Action	Insight
Investors	Also, gauge whether they are in it for the long haul and are not fair-weather friends.
	Assemble a diverse Board, not people who are your self-image. Turn over the Board members at different stages of your business development. It's not 'one size fits all'.
	Investors are clearly in it for a positive return. However, this does not mean that you should only share the positive news with them. It is far better to share your challenges too and keep them apprised of how you are addressing them. The investors may have valuable insights that they can share with you, based on their experiences and perspectives.
Contractors and employees	Once you've reached the limits of your own capacity, you need to hire and delegate.
	The more passionate you are about your vision, the more likely you believe everyone is on board with you. Do not just assume that your vision is well understood and embraced. Have open conversations to check that everyone on the team is aligned with what you are trying to achieve.
	Take time to get to know your contractors and employees; their expectations, fears and standards of practice. Ask explicitly and do not assume. Clarify, check-in frequently and recap to confirm their understanding.
	If you assume that your employees or contractors are only in it for the pay, you

Action	Insight
	will miss out on all they have to offer, such as loyalty, contribution and ideas.
	Read the terms and conditions of all contracts. Be open to renegotiating and setting new terms that are more applicable to the unfolding situation.
	If you are bringing people together from different backgrounds, check their mindset and how it differs from yours.
Speed	In your enthusiasm and ambition, you may move too fast. Check whose timetable you are working towards; has it been set by your investors, employees, family, or your own self-imposed deadlines fuelled by your self-identity or reputation?
Focus	Pace yourself; take time to make time. Otherwise you may end up with misunderstandings, leading to frustration, waste and having to make good or remediate.
	Set boundaries on your time and do similar tasks by blocks. Multi-tasking does not work for complex tasks. Read the details when you can focus on them, not when you are on the hop.
Plan B	Unless you are looking for a quick flip to monetise your idea, you may not have considered an exit strategy.

Action	Insight
Self-identity	Thinking through the issues and where there are vulnerabilities in your strategy is just plain sense.
	If you have a 'fixed' mindset you see failure as a blot on your reputation or status. If you have a 'growth' mindset you can separate your identity from the failure of your business. You recognise that it is not you personally who failed, but how you did it that failed. You will learn to adjust your strategy and make a comeback.
Self-care	You will be faced with innumerable decisions to make. Making them when you are exhausted, distracted, resentful or angry will lead to sub-optimal decisions.
	You will have situations where you have to work extremely long hours. However, this cannot become your norm. It cannot be sustained because the quality of your decision-making, relationships and health will deteriorate.
	Cultivate practices to improve your self-awareness, to take stock, refresh and rejuvenate, such as meditation, self-compassion, getting out into nature, listening to music, art, sports and leisure activities with your family and friends.
	Listen to your body and be aware of your mental health. Take notice of and relieve strained eyes, hunched shoulders, a tight chest or aches in your lower back. Do not just 'push through the pain'. You are fooling

Action	Insight
	yourself that you will make the best choices under these conditions.
	Record what energises you and inspires your creativity. In a complex, unpredictable and fast-changing world, having only one solution is the enemy.
	Experimentation and multiple options will generate the best outcomes.

Notes

Introduction

1. The humble pie had its origins in early medieval England. It was a pie filled with offal and meat from deer and other animals. The pastry was inedible – it was made as 'packaging' for carrying the pie and meant to be discarded. There are some references to the aristocracy eating such a pie one day a year to remind them of their good fortune. Nowadays to 'eat humble pie' is to be humiliated and forced to admit error or wrongdoing.

2. See Jennifer Garvey Berger's *Unlocking Leadership Mindtraps: How to Thrive in Complexity* (Stanford, CA: Stanford University Press, 2019). Entrepreneurs are leaders and this brief book is a very useful resource on how to free yourself from set patterns of thinking.

3. See "Intrepreneurs and Entrepreneurs" by Emma Isaacs in *The Huffington Post* at huffpost.com.

Slice 2: Preparation and sifting

1. To learn more about Peer Advisory Circles, see the blog post, "The Value of Collective Wisdom" on SylvanaCaloni.com.

2. Read more about testing and modifying your concept and taking care not to fall in love with your solution when there is not a demand for it. See the blog post, "Test, learn and tweak" on SylvanaCaloni.com.

Slice 3: Improvising the recipe

1. Read Alan Sieler in *Coaching to the Human Soul*, Volume II, p64 (Victoria: Newfield Australia, 2007) for more about how our bodies, brains, logic and emotions are interconnected.

2. 'Mapping across' is a term used in Neuro-Linguistic Programming. To explore further, watch *Mapping Across – an NLP technique using submodalities* on NLP-Mentor.com.

3. For a comprehensive discussion of how the various parts of our brain work, interrelate and make sense, read Keiron Sparrowhawk's *Executive Function: Cognitive Fitness for Business* (London: LID Publishing, 2016).

4. Rafael Echeverria wrote a seminal paper on this subject – *Four Basic Moods About Life* (unpublished paper, The Newfield Network, 2001).

Slice 4: Kneading the ingredients

1. Read Richard Barrett's article, "Fundamentals of Cultural Transformation: Implementing Whole

Systems Change" in the Resource Library at ValuesCentre.com.

2. To complete a free Personal Values Assessment (PVA) go to valuescentre.com.

3. This exercise is adapted from the self-development exercises found in the Barrett Values personal assessment referenced above.

Slice 5: The binding agents – relationships

1. Steven MR Covey coined the term "Smart Trust" in his book, *The Speed of Trust: The One Thing That Changes Everything* (London: Simon & Schuster, 2006).

2. See Reid Hoffman and Ben Casnocha, *The Start-Up of You*, p22 (London: Random House, 2012).

3. Judith E Glaser had a very successful career, spanning decades working with remarkable Chief Executive Officers such as Angela Ahrendts, who was responsible for the reinvigoration of the fashion group, Burberry, and Bob Lutz, who 'recharged' Exide, the battery technologies company. Judith brought together her body of work integrating insights from neuroscience in her best-selling book, *Conversational Intelligence: How Great Leaders Build Trust and Get Extraordinary Results* (Brookline, MA: Bibliomotion, 2014).

4. To learn more about the 'Tell-Sell-Yell Syndrome' see Judith E Glaser, *ibid*, pp87-89.

5. Steven MR Covey, *ibid*, pp287-299.

Slice 6: The folding of Humble Pie

1. For a more extensive discussion see "Plan Continuation Bias and Decision-Making" by P Chisambara, 1ˢᵗ July 2019, on ERPMInsights.com.

2. See CS Dweck, *Mindset: How You Can Fulfil Your Potential* (London: Constable & Robinson, 2006).

3. Reid Hoffman and Ben Casnocha, *ibid*, pp. 20-21.

4. There is a lot of literature on the importance of our bodies or 'soma' in how we behave and respond. See for example the works of Amanda Blake, Pete Hamill, and Richard Strozzi-Heckler in the bibliography.

5. Robert Dunham, *Managing Capacity, Managing Promises, Building Your Future p1* (Course notes, Coaching Excellence in Organizations™, 2008). Dunham also shared his work on a Newfield Network learning call entitled, *Managing Overwhelm: The Leader's Dilemma, The Coach's Opportunity*, 11ᵗʰ December 2007.

Selected Bibliography

Books

Barrett, Richard. *The New Leadership Paradigm* (Lulu.com, 2011)

Berger, Jennifer Garvey. *Unlocking Leadership Mindtraps: How to Thrive in Complexity* (Stanford, CA: Stanford University Press, 2019)

Blake, Amanda. *Your Body is Your Brain: Leverage Your Somatic Intelligence to Find Purpose, Build Resilience, Deepen Relationships and Lead More Powerfully* (USA: Trokay Press/Embright LLC, 2018)

Collins, Jim. *Good to Great* (London: Random House Business Books, 2001)

Denning, Peter J, and Dunham, Robert. *The Innovator's Way: Essential Practices for Successful Innovation* (Cambridge, MA: The MIT Press, 2010)

Dweck, Carol S. *Mindset: How You Can Fulfil Your Potential* (London: Constable & Robinson, 2006)

Glaser, Judith E. *Conversational Intelligence: How Great Leaders Build Trust and Get Extraordinary Results* (Brookline, MA: Bibliomotion, 2014)

Hamill, Pete. *Embodied Leadership: The Somatic Approach to Developing Your Leadership* (London: Kogan Page, 2013)

Hoffman, Reid and Casnocha, Ben. *The Start-up of You: Adapt to the Future, Invest in Yourself and Transform Your Future* (London: Random House, 2012)

McGee, Harold. *On Food and Cooking: The Science and Lore of the Kitchen* (New York: Macmillan Publishing, 1984)

Newby, Dan and Núñez, Lucy. *The Unopened Gift: A Primer in Emotional Literacy* (USA: Daniel Newby, 2017)

Sisodia, Rajendra J, Wolfe, David B and Sheth, Jagdish N. *Firms of Endearment: How World-Class Companies Profit from Passion and Purpose* (New Jersey: Prentice Hall, 2007)

Sparrowhawk, Keiron. *Executive Function: Cognitive Fitness for Business* (London: LID Publishing, 2016)

Strozzi-Heckler, Richard. *The Leadership Dojo: Build Your Foundation as an Exemplary Leader* (Berkeley, CA: Frog Ltd, 2007)

Williams, Alan and Whybrow, Alison. *The 31 Practices: Release the Power of Your Organisation's Values Every Day* (London: LID Publishing, 2013)

Articles

Caloni, Sylvana. "Vision is Not Enough for Business Success" (SylvanaCaloni.com, 14th February 2016)

Caloni, Sylvana. "Are You Response-able?" (SylvanaCaloni.com, 14th February 2016)

Chisambara, Peter. "Plan Continuation Bias and Decision Making" (ERPMInsights.com, 1st July 2019)

Appendix

Humble Brags: Paul's three favourite pie recipes

In these recipes we suggest you use ready-made store-bought puff pastry. Our secret pastry recipe is still a secret!

To ensure you make a perfect pie each time, follow these Humble rules:

- When you make the pie filling, leave it in the fridge overnight for all the ingredients to blend together and release their full flavour.

- *Never* put warm or hot pie filling on to the raw pastry in the pie tin. Otherwise the pastry will become soggy and chewy.

- All recipes are for four small individual pies of about 250g each. We use 11cm round pie tins.

- Roll out two pieces of pastry per pie tin – place one layer of thinly rolled pastry on the bottom and sides of the pie tin and another on top.

- Do not blind-bake the pastry, use it raw.

- Use a little milk or egg wash on the pastry cover before baking so it comes out with an attractive glossy top.

- Cook from thawed or frozen at 200°C (180°C fan)/350°F/Gas Mark 4 for about 40 minutes until they are golden brown and the filling is really hot.

- Leave them to rest for a few minutes after taking them out of the oven and before removing them from the tin.

- If you are not going to eat them immediately, they freeze really well – you can freeze them when they are at oven-ready stage (without the milk or egg wash) or after baking.

Aussie minced beef pie

This is an Australian pie. No veggies! If you really want to, you can add some peas and chopped carrots.

Ingredients
ready-made puff pastry (approximately 100g per pie)
500g lean minced beef
1 tsp plain flour
1 tbsp olive oil
1 large onion, peeled and finely chopped
1 tbsp tomato purée
1 clove of peeled garlic, minced
1 crumbled beef stock cube
1/2 tsp ground nutmeg
salt and white pepper to taste
1 tsp cornflour (optional)

Method

1. In a dry, medium-size frying pan over a medium heat, brown the minced beef with the plain flour and set aside. Pour off any excess fat then return to the heat and add the onions and minced garlic to the pan. Sprinkle the ground nutmeg over the mince and sauté with 1 tablespoon of olive oil until the onions are translucent but not coloured.

2. Add the crumbled stock cube and tomato purée and season. Mix all the ingredients together and

cook gently for 45 minutes, stirring occasionally, until the mixture thickens. Add a little cornflour, if required, to thicken or a little water to loosen it up if necessary. Once it is cooked, put the filling in a covered bowl and leave overnight in the fridge.

3. To assemble the pies, lightly grease the pie tins and fit each with enough pastry so that some of it hangs over the sides of the tin. Overfill each pie tin with the beef mixture and place the pastry lid on top, again ensuring there is some pastry hanging over the side.

4. The pastry will shrink a little when it is cooked so when you trim the excess pastry around the pie tin, leave a little bit extra on the edges. Press the lid and bottom parts of the pastry together using the prongs of a fork to seal them. Pierce the lid a few times with a sharp knife or a fork in any pattern you like. This not only makes the pie look attractive, it allows the steam from baking to escape so the pastry does not become soggy.

5. If you want to freeze the pies, now is the time to do it. Wrap them in cling film to stop the pastry drying out and you're done.

6. When you are ready to cook them (whether freshly made or from frozen) brush with a little

milk or egg wash, bake at 200°C (180°C fan)/350°F/Gas Mark 4 for around 40 minutes until the pastry is golden and the filling is piping hot.

7. Let the pies rest for a few minutes, flip them over (careful, they will be hot), tap the bottom of the tin with a spoon and the pie will pop out.

These pies are great with ketchup, mashed potato and green peas.

Spicy Mediterranean harissa pie

Ingredients

ready-made puff pastry (approximately 100g per pie)

1 medium aubergine

2 small courgettes

2 bell peppers (any colour), stems and seeds removed

2 ripe vine tomatoes

1 medium red onion, peeled

2 small cloves of peeled garlic, minced

splash of red wine vinegar

2 tbsp olive oil

1 tbsp rose harissa

a little torn basil

salt and white pepper to taste

Method

1. To make the ratatouille filling, cut all the vegetables into medium-size chunks. Warm the olive oil in a medium-size saucepan, add the rose harissa, the garlic and the seasoning. Cook gently for 30 minutes, stirring occasionally, until the smell is fragrant and the ingredients retain a little 'bite'. (You do not want wet mush.) Once the ratatouille is cooked, put it in a covered bowl and leave overnight in the fridge for the flavours to come together.

2. To assemble the pies, lightly grease the pie tins and fit each with enough pastry so that some of it hangs over the sides of the tin. Overfill each pie tin with the ratatouille mixture and place the pastry lid on top, again ensuring there is some pastry hanging over the side.

3. The pastry will shrink a little when it is cooked, so when you trim the excess pastry around the pie tin leave a little bit extra on the edges. Press the lid and bottom parts of the pastry together using the prongs of a fork to seal them. Pierce the lid a few times with a sharp knife or a fork in any pattern you like. This not only makes the pie look attractive, it allows the steam from baking to escape so the pastry does not become soggy.

4. If you want to freeze the pies, now is the time to do it. Wrap them in cling film to stop the pastry drying out and you're done.

5. When you are ready to bake them (whether freshly made or from frozen), brush the pastry lid with a little milk or egg wash, bake at 200°C (180°C fan)/350°F/Gas Mark 4 for around 40 minutes until the pastry is golden and the filling is piping hot.

6. When done, let them rest for a few minutes, flip them over (careful, they will be hot), tap the

bottom of the tin with a spoon and the pie will pop out.

These pies are great served on their own or with a salad.

Chicken, avocado and brie pie

Ingredients

ready-made puff pastry (approximately 100g per pie)
400g boneless, skinless chicken thighs, poached, diced
60g Maris Piper potatoes, peeled and diced
1 avocado, cut into four thin slices per pie
1 brie, cut into four thin slices per pie
chicken stock for poaching
salt and white pepper to taste

For the white sauce:

1 tsp Dijon mustard
1 tbsp unsalted butter
2 tsp plain flour
splash of white wine
25ml double cream
25ml whole milk

Method

1. To make the white sauce, first gently melt the butter and add the flour, stirring constantly in a small saucepan. Take care not to let the mixture colour. When smooth and fully blended, add the mustard, white wine, double cream and whole milk, stirring constantly over low to medium heat. The sauce should be thick, but you should still be able to pour it. Transfer to a medium mixing bowl.

2. In a separate pan, poach the diced chicken and potato in some chicken stock. Once cooked, drain and add to the bowl of white sauce. Season with salt and pepper to taste, stir together, cover, and leave overnight in the fridge for the flavours to come together.

3. To assemble the pies, lightly grease the pie tins and fit each one with enough pastry so that some of it hangs over the sides of the tin. Fill each pie tin three-quarters full with the chicken and potato mixture (do not overfill) and place four slices each of brie and avocado on top of the mixture. It is very important to seal the pie as quickly as possible to stop the avocado from oxidizing and turning black, so immediately place the pastry lid on top, again ensuring there is some pastry hanging over the side. The pastry will shrink a little when it is cooked so when you trim the excess pastry around the pie tin leave a little bit extra on the edges.

4. Press the lid on to the bottom part of the pastry using the prongs of a fork to seal the pie. Pierce the lid a few times with a sharp knife or a fork in any pattern you like. This not only makes the pie look attractive, it allows the steam from baking to escape so the pastry does not become soggy.

5. If you want to freeze the pies, now is the time to do it. Wrap them in cling film to stop the pastry drying out and you're done.

6. When you are ready to bake them (whether freshly made or from frozen), brush the pastry lid with a little milk or egg wash, bake at 200°C (180°C fan)/350°F/Gas Mark 4 for around 40 minutes until the pastry is golden and the filling is piping hot.

7. When done, let them rest for a few minutes, flip them over (careful, they will be hot), tap the bottom of the tin with a spoon and the pie will pop out.

These pies are great served with a mixed salad.

Acknowledgements

During the course of putting pen to paper, we had conversations with many people from a broad range of disciplines to get their feedback and make sure that what we were doing was helpful and relevant. We are very grateful to each and every one of you – your commentary has had a huge, positive influence on this project.

We would like to give a special mention to Helen Oakwater, Ann Deaton and Dan Newby for their advice on the discipline of writing.

We facilitate Peer Advisory Circles and for several years they were graciously hosted by Marian Bloodworth, Employment Partner of the London-based boutique law firm, Kemp Little. Hundreds of early-stage entrepreneurs and executives transitioning from a corporate career trusted us to share their challenges, aspirations and successes and to learn from the collective wisdom of the participants. In particular, we are grateful to Alan Williams, Christine Brown-Quinn, Samuel T Reddy, Cherron Inko-Tariah MBE, Jim Rees and Keiron Sparrowhawk who, also as successful authors, inspired and encouraged us.

We were energised by the imagination and vision of the aspiring entrepreneurs we mentor at the London School of Economics and Regent's University London.

Many thanks to our editor, Katia Hadidian, for her insights, expertise and enthusiasm. Also to Samsang Kelsang, a wonderfully creative graphic artist who designed the images that so effectively communicate our ideas. All errors and omissions remain our responsibility.

Lastly, our gratitude to the Board of Advisors, Board of Directors, shareholders and employees who passed through the doors of Humble Pie.

About the Authors

 **Paul O'Donnell** is an investment banker turned business consultant with decades of experience in Australia, Asia, the UK and USA in strategic and operational leadership, and business development for multinational financial institutions. He is also a serial entrepreneur, advises owners of small to medium-sized enterprises and mentors students of entrepreneurship.

 **Sylvana Caloni** is a leadership coach who works with clients internationally. In her early career in global financial markets she was a bond dealer, equity analyst and fund manager. She blends the insights from the fast-paced financial services world and the latest training on learning and development to enable entrepreneurs, executives and self-starting individuals to become more self-aware, more effective and more successful.

If you would like more information on our consulting services, coaching, mentoring, peer advisory circles and training you can contact us at:

paul@lisdoonvarna.co.uk
linkedin.com/in/paulmodonnell
@pododonnell

sylvana@sylvanacaloni.com
sylvanacaloni.com
linkedin.com/in/sylvanacaloni
@sylvanacaloni

Printed in Great Britain
by Amazon